NATIVE AMERICAN COOKING

NATIVE AMERICAN COOKING

FOODS OF THE SOUTHWEST INDIAN NATIONS

LOIS ELLEN FRANK

WITH
CYNTHIA J. FRANK

Culinary Advisor:
JOHN SEDLAR

Food Stylists:
SUSAN SOUTHCOTT AND NORMAN STEWART

DESIGN BY MARILU LOPEZ

WINGS BOOKS
NEW YORK • AVENEL, NEW JERSEY

Author's note: Foods in this book may be unfamiliar, especially to those who have never been to the Southwest. I urge readers to be absolutely certain to identify wild edibles before eating them and to adhere to any special instructions or warnings I have included in the recipes. I also suggest that inexperienced hunters purchase game meats from a butcher, as wild animals may carry disease.

Copyright ©1991 by Lois Ellen Frank

This 1995 edition is published by Wings Books, distributed by Random House Value Publishing, Inc., 40 Engelhard Avenue, Avenel, New Jersey 07001, by arrangement with Clarkson Potter/Publishers.

Random House
New York • Toronto • London • Sydney • Auckland

Printed and bound in China

Library of Congress Cataloging–in–Publication Data

Frank, Lois Ellen.
    Native American cooking / Lois Ellen Frank
    with Cynthia J. Frank.
        p.   cm.
    Originally published: New York : C.N. Potter, c1991.
    Includes Index.
    ISBN 0–517–14750–5
    1. Indian cookery, 2. Cookery, American—
Southwestern style. 3. Indians of North America—Food.
I. Frank, Cynthia J. II. Title.
TX715.F8355 1995
641.59'297079—dc20   95–16670
                                             CIP

8 7 6 5 4 3 2 1

To Ernst Haas,
for starting me on this journey
and giving me the courage
to create a book from the poetry
within my heart, and
to all of the Native American
people who graciously shared
their ancient food traditions and
opened their homes and
hearts to help make this book
a reality

ACKNOWLEDGMENTS

Many more people than I ever could have imagined were needed to help me in the completion of this book. I am so grateful to each and every one of them for their support.

First and foremost, I would like to thank John Sedlar, co-owner and chef of Saint Estèphe, his restaurant in Manhattan Beach, California. John, without whom I could not have produced this book, shared with me his culinary expertise and worked diligently with me day in and day out on the adaptation of the recipes.

My sister, Cynthia J. Frank, came into this project after it had begun but worked with me until the very end. She followed me around the Southwest with the computer, writing and rewriting the manuscript from start to finish and helping me to organize my thoughts so that they could be put into words.

Susan Southcott and Norman Stewart are two of the most talented food stylists I have ever worked with. Their creative imaginations helped to produce the wonderfully vivid style and presentation of the food in the photographs. They, too, traveled with me to many of the reservations for on-location shoots, bringing with them their imagination and ingenuity under even the most adverse conditions.

Norman Kolpas, whom I first met as a guest speaker at a cookbook writing class at UCLA, helped me with the conception and format of the book and with the introduction. He gave me the confidence and final push to go to New York and sell the idea of a cookbook on Native American cuisine.

Steve Garcia, co-owner of Saint Estèphe, not only allowed but hospitably welcomed me to spend many days, nights, and weekends in the restaurant's kitchen as I worked on modifications of the recipes. I never once saw him without a smile on his face.

And, of course, thanks to the entire kitchen staff at Saint Estèphe. They invariably cleared a generous work space for me, even during the busiest restaurant hours. I also thank them for tasting and critiquing many recipes.

Dovida Treiman, Sue Tallon, and Christine Stafford, my faithful assistants, all put in long hours of editing, labeling, mounting, and organizing incredible amounts of film.

Julie Dennis, my studio partner at the time this book was in production, gave me her support while I was working in the studio, and took the photograph of John and me.

Mona Enfield and her entire family welcomed me into their beautiful home in Santa Fe on many of my visits to the area, enabling me to be in close proximity to the pueblos and reservations of the Southwest.

Barbara Lowenstein, my literary agent, was tireless in making all the arrangements for the publication of this book.

To Marilu Lopez, thank you for your sympathetic and beautiful design. To the entire staff of Clarkson N. Potter, especially Carol Southern, Carolyn Hart Gavin, Isolde Motley, Howard Klein, Amy Schuler, Amy Boorstein, Lisa Lawley, and Joy Sikorski, thank you for making a dream become a reality.

There were also many gallery owners who, through goodness and generosity, allowed me to use numerous artifacts for the photographs and offered their premises for on-location shots.

I would like to express my deepest gratitude to the following Native American people who opened up their hearts and their homes, both on and off the reservations. I will cherish their friendship forever.
• Juanita Tiger Kavena and her wonderful family — Wilmer, Tracy, Maria, Tita, Chibbon, Alisha, Natyo, and Lisa — from the Hopi Reservation • E. J. Satala, his parents Granny and Grampa, his sister Hazel, his son Spike, and all the members of the Honanie family; and Genevieve Kaursgowva, all from the Hopi Reservation • Richard and Margie Mermejo from Picuris Pueblo • Ann Taliman from Santa Clara Pueblo • Charlotte and Phillip Titla from San Carlos Apache Reservation • Del Mar Boni, from San Carlos Apache Reservation and Gila River Pima Reservation • Sarah H. Adeky and her family from Ramah, Navajo Tribe

And finally, I would like to show my appreciation to the following tribes, pueblos, and people for their participation in and contributions to this book:
• Acoma Pueblo, Acomita, New Mexico • Cochiti Pueblo, Cochiti, New Mexico (John Bowannie and Lena Jaramillo) • Havasupai Nation, Arizona • Hopi Nation, Arizona • Hualapai Reservation, Peach Springs, Arizona (Lucille Watahomigie) • Isleta Pueblo, Isleta, New Mexico (Betty Johnson and Maria Elena Roybal) • Jemez Pueblo, Jemez, New Mexico (Inez Toya and Angie Trujillo) • Mescalero Apache Tribe, Mescalero, New Mexico • Mountain Ute Tribe, Tawoac, Colorado • Navajo Nation, Window Rock, Arizona • Papago Nation, Arizona • Picuris Pueblo, Penasco, New Mexico (Margaret Archuleta and Mary Ann Martinez) • Pima Nation, Gila River Reservation, Arizona • Ramah Navajo Tribe, Ramah, New Mexico • San Carlos Apache Tribe, San Carlos, Arizona • San Ildefonso Pueblo, Santa Fe, New Mexico • San Juan Pueblo, San Juan, New Mexico • Santa Ana Pueblo, San Ysidro, New Mexico • Santa Clara Pueblo, Española, New Mexico (Frank Gutierrez, Janice Naranjo, and Tessie Naranjo) • Southern Ute Tribe, Ignacio, Colorado (Dr. Donald S. Heany and Annabel Eagle) • Taos Pueblo, Taos, New Mexico (Lillian Romero) • Tesuque Pueblo, Tesuque, New Mexico (Sue Dorame) • White River Apache Tribe, White River, Arizona, (Gina Marie Thomas) • Zia Pueblo, San Ysidro, New Mexico • Zuni Pueblo, Zuni, New Mexico

CONTENTS

FOREWORD

In the fall of 1982, when the chile crop was ripening near my hometown of Santa Fe, New Mexico, I first began to experiment with native foods of the American Southwest. I returned to Saint Estèphe, the restaurant I opened with Steve Garcia in Manhattan Beach, California, with fifteen cases of chiles and tested them in every course but dessert. The result, for me, was a kind of cooking I named "Modern Southwest Cuisine" — a combination of traditional ingredients, my training in classic French cuisine, and the new, light, modern approach to cooking.

Since that time, I have watched interest in the foods of the Southwest grow to the point where dozens upon dozens of chefs across the country are offering their own interpretations of Native American recipes. What continues to surprise me is the flexibility, the adaptability of America's first cuisine. When a young photographer named Lois Ellen Frank was first introduced to me by our mutual friend Norman Kolpas in the beginning of 1987, I was intrigued to learn that she was embarking on a study of southwestern cooking in its purest, most unadulterated form — in the age-old ways it is being prepared by the Indian nations today. When Lois asked me to consult with her and help her adapt the recipes she was gathering so that they could be prepared by modern cooks who don't have access to adobe ovens or open fires, I saw a rare opportunity to learn a

great deal more about the cuisine that was an integral part of my own culinary background.

Lois collected many traditional recipes from Native American tribes all over the Southwest. She then brought them to me to help her adapt the concept of the recipes to suit the modern kitchen and current nutritional standards. She would then test the recipes to decide if they were consistent with the vision she had for her book. Some of the recipes Lois gathered were incredibly simple: One stew, for example, called for just three ingredients — lamb, hominy, and water. To such recipes, I usually recommended she add seasonings to contemporary taste without in any way altering the direct simplicity of the dish. But, fascinatingly, many of the recipes stood on their own, requiring little if any adaptation. The only major development you'll find in them is a modern sense of decorative presentation that nevertheless utilizes traditional southwestern symbols, textures, and colors.

Lois Ellen Frank is an extraordinary photographer and an inspired observer of the American Southwest, its people, and their food. I feel fortunate to have worked with her in the preparation of this book.

John Sedlar
Saint Estèphe
Manhattan Beach, California

HOW THIS BOOK BEGAN

When I graduated from Brooks Institute of Photography in Santa Barbara, I was asked to give a speech at the commencement. With this special opportunity, I wanted to reach out to every person there and explain my feelings about photography: how the images we produce should be positive and productive and, if possible, influence generations to come.

After I spoke, the renowned photographer Ernst Haas gave a speech. Although I had never met him before, his words seemed to come from my heart and his visions from my eyes. It was then that I knew that this man would be not only an acquaintance, but a mentor and true friend.

As I got to know Ernst better, he encouraged me to share many of my own visions with him. To my dismay, he frowned upon some of the work I was doing. "If this is not the poetry from inside your heart," he asked, "then what is it? Is this the message you want to give to others?"

There were no answers. After years of educating myself in a field I deeply loved, I was completely lost.

Ernst believed that in order to express your visions through an art form you must allow your childlike, unin-hibited feelings to surface. And, you must be able to cap-ture those images in pure form. "Quite often," he explained to me with distaste, "I see people photographing things

that they don't necessarily care about, just to make money. And then when they finally reach a point in their lives when they have time to be creative, they have forgotten what it is they wanted to express in the first place."

And so I began to search for the message I wanted to convey through my photography. I knew I had to look within myself. I began to have dreams: I saw myself doing very simple things, grinding corn, making baskets, and planting seeds. I've always tried to be in touch with the earth and have been especially interested in people who are; also, perhaps because my grandfather was a Kiowa Indian, I have always found myself deeply interested in the Native American culture. As I told Ernst about these visions and feelings, he pushed me even further. He knew that I must elaborate on these emotions and create beautiful images from them.

I have now spent several years visiting and living on many of the southwestern Indian reservations. I have learned from the elders where to find, how to harvest, and how to prepare Native American foods. They have taught me traditional methods of cooking as well as new approaches. In addition, they have given me permission to photograph their food rituals, a rare privilege.

In September of 1986, while I was on my first trip to the Hopi reservation, Ernst died unexpectedly of a stroke. The news of his death left me with a great feeling of emptiness. I know Ernst cannot be by my side to see this book published, but his spirit lives within me. Every day, as I have worked on this book, a part of his wisdom continues to thrive. His way of looking at things will live forever.

Lois Ellen Frank

INTRODUCTION

To the Native Americans of the Southwest, food is more than physical sustenance. The people of the southwestern tribes live in close harmony with the natural world; their religions are based on a belief that the gods are embodied in the forces of nature and in all living things. So every food, whether plant or animal, is considered sacred. And the acts of hunting, growing, gathering, cooking, and eating take on a spiritual aspect akin to prayer.

Visiting and living in the Southwest season after season, I've witnessed firsthand the many ways in which the daily tasks that revolve around food take on sacred meaning. The planting and growing seasons of the Hopi — a settled people who are masters of agriculture — are integral to their religious calendar. Not surprisingly, the eating habits of the southwestern tribes follow the seasons closely. As a result, unlike the European approach to dining, in which meals are composed of several courses that embrace all the basic food groups, traditional Southwest Native American meals tend to rely on the few staples available at any particular time of year, so there is a deep respect for food.

To reflect such an approach to eating, this book is organized not by courses but rather by the main categories of food Southwest natives eat. There are separate chapters on corn, the most important staple; vine-grown vegetables and

fruits such as squashes and tomatoes; wild fruits and greens; legumes; game birds, meats, and fish; and finally, breads. Within each of these sections, you'll find recipes for a number of different courses — appetizers, soups, salads, main courses, side dishes, desserts — from which you can compose a more conventional meal.

To offer an overall picture of the region, I have chosen not to separate the recipes by tribe. Thus you'll find a variety of influences throughout the book: recipes that derive from the sophisticated farming techniques of the Hopi and other Pueblo tribes; recipes that include fish, from the tribes that settled along the Rio Grande in northern New Mexico; recipes that reflect the hunting-and-gathering diets of the Navajo and Apache tribes; recipes featuring cactus, a special staple of the Pima and Papago peoples.

All of the recipes have been adapted to the modern kitchen; wherever possible, I've given advice on how to find special ingredients and suggested more common ingredients you can substitute. Where necessary, I've also adapted the recipes — with the guidance of leading southwestern chef John Sedlar — to contemporary tastes and dietary habits. This, I believe, is a valid approach to the Native American food of the Southwest; it reflects a natural trend in the cuisine that began in the last century, as Hispanic and Anglo settlers moved to the region and brought with them their own cooking methods and ingredients such as beef, pork, wheat, sugar, and dairy products. Any adaptations I have made have been done with the sole purpose of making the recipes in this book accessible to as wide an audience as possible; throughout, I have always striven to respect the inherent qualities of the Native American recipes.

CORN

Corn is, and has been for thousands of years, one of the most important foods in the Native American diet. Considered to be the essence of life, corn holds a magical sacredness for the people. In fact, many ceremonial dances are held in which prayers are offered to the Corn Mother spirit.

Corn was originally cultivated thousands of years ago in the Southwest. The first variety grown did not require irrigation, making it perfect for the people to cultivate in the dry, arid regions of the Southwest. The seeds were planted up to eighteen inches deep so they could obtain water for germination. As the young corn plants grew, the healthiest shoots pushed aside the weaker ones on their long journey to the earth's surface, producing plenty of thriving corn for harvest. "Dry-farming," as this method is called, is still used by some tribes; many other methods of growing corn have also been developed by Native Americans.

Several different varieties and colors of corn — including blue, white, red, yellow, and speckled — are used by Native Americans today. Blue corn, which varies in color from pale blue to almost black, is considered one of the most important corn crops. It is used primarily in making baked goods, stews, stuffings, dumplings, and beverages. Recent studies indicate that this variety of corn may have more nutritional value than other types. White corn is still a major crop on many reservations and pueblos. It is used in prayer offerings and for making hominy and cornmeal flour, which is utilized in many traditional recipes. Red corn, ranging in color from light red to deep maroon, is used for baked goods, for stews, and, traditionally, for dye. It is also used to make parched corn, that is, corn that has been roasted so that the kernels are crunchy. Yellow corn is used in stews and is ground into flour or meal for baking. It is often substituted for white corn in cooking because of its greater availability. Speckled corn, which is a combination of all the colors of corn, is used for all kinds of cooking.

In the past, to help themselves endure the long, harsh winters, Native Americans dried much of their corn just after harvest, laying up enough to last through two cropless winters. Today it is still common during harvest season to see corn hanging in strands outside adobe houses in the Southwest. (There are two methods of drying corn. One is simply to string fresh corn cobs, in their husks, on long yucca threads and hang them outside for several weeks. The other is to bake the cobs before drying, a process that enhances the corn's flavors.)

Some of the dishes in this chapter are presented in their traditional form as they have been served for many generations. Others I have adapted to make them easier and quicker to prepare, without compromising the integrity of the traditional recipe. Still other recipes are my own interpretation of the foods as I have experienced them during my travels to the Native American pueblos and reservations. All of the recipes, however, illustrate the great importance of corn to Native Americans.

There is a simplicity and subtleness to the flavor of corn that makes it uniquely suitable for use in so many diverse and creative ways, in both centuries-old and modern recipes.

Indian Hominy

Almost every tribe and pueblo throughout the Southwest region uses hominy as a base for many Native American dishes. Made from dried corn in a variety of colors, hominy can be eaten as is, canned, dried and stored for winter use (the dried hominy must be soaked in water first and then cooked), ground into a meal and used for corn tortillas or tamales, or added to stews.

When sold in Hispanic markets, hominy — canned or dried — is called *pozole*. In certain regions of New Mexico, *pozole* can also refer to a cooked dish (page 22).

2 cups dried corn kernels
10 cups water
1 cup culinary ash (see Note) or 2 tablespoons baking soda

Soak the dried corn overnight in a bowl filled with the cold water.

The following day, put the corn and water into an enameled pot. (Because the culinary ash reacts with metal, hominy must be processed in an enameled pot.) Cover and bring to a boil over high heat.

When the water begins to boil, stir in the culinary ash. At this point, the ash will intensify the color of the kernels.

Cover and reduce heat. Simmer over low heat for about 5½ hours, until the hulls are loose and the corn returns to its original color. Stir occasionally and replenish with enough water to cover the corn when necessary, or it will dry out and burn on the bottom.

Under cold running water, rub corn between fingers to remove hulls, which should be discarded. Drain corn in a colander.

To dry hominy in the traditional manner, spread the cooked and hulled corn on an open-weave basket or screen and place in full sun, turning the kernels every few hours, until completely dry. Alternatively, place the kernels on a sheet pan in a gas oven with the pilot light on, or in an electric oven on the lowest setting, turning every few hours until dry. (Check by breaking open a kernel: If there is any moisture inside, keep drying.) Once properly dried, hominy will keep almost indefinitely without spoilage.

Makes 5 cups cooked or 3 cups dried hominy

NOTE: Culinary ash is made from burning the wood of certain trees until there is only ash left. Many types of trees and bushes found throughout the Southwest can be used; the Navajos use juniper primarily and the Hopis use green plants such as *suwvi* or *chamisa* bushes. The green twigs, when burned, pro-

POZOLE, *with hominy as its base, is a very common traditional dish in New Mexico.*

duce an ash with a high mineral content. When used in cooking, it increases the food's nutritional value.

When culinary ash is mixed with boiling water and corn the alkaline level in the ash reacts with the corn and changes it to a more intense color. After the water has cooled, the corn changes again — to something close to its original color.

If you are in an area where culinary ash is difficult to obtain, baking soda can be used as a substitute, although it doesn't have the high nutritional content of ash. Substitute 2 tablespoons baking soda for 1 cup ash. (See Source Guide, page 153.)

Pozole
(STEWED HOMINY)

Pozole is a simple, rustic stew common throughout the pueblos in New Mexico and parts of Arizona. Made from dried hominy, salt pork, spices, and dried red chiles, the stew is usually cooked in large quantities. It is customarily eaten during pueblo feast days, when the pueblo's patron saint is celebrated, and on New Year's Day, when a hearty meal for cold weather is welcome.

The stew is traditionally served with a variety of condiments. It tastes especially good with Red Chile Sauce (page 26), freshly roasted diced green chiles (page 62–63), chile pequín, and any of the Indian breads.

1½ cups dried Indian Hominy (page 21)
6 quarts water
½ pound pork rind, cubed
2 pounds pork ribs
2 dried New Mexico red chile pods, seeded, stemmed and torn into 6 pieces
1 small onion, chopped
2 garlic cloves, chopped
1 teaspoon fresh oregano leaves, finely chopped
1 teaspoon *azafrán* (Native American saffron; see Note, page 83)

Soak the hominy overnight in 1 quart water.

The following day, drain and discard the water. Place the hominy in a large pot filled with the remaining 5 quarts water and cook over low to medium heat about 4 hours, until the kernels burst and are puffy and tender.

Add more water, if necessary, to cover the kernels. Add the pork rind and ribs, red chiles, onion, and garlic and cook another 1½ hours, until the meat is tender and falling off the bone. Add the oregano and *azafrán* and cook another 15 minutes.

Remove the meat from the ribs and discard the bones. Return the meat to the pot. Serve hot.

Makes 3 cups pozole

BAKING SWEET CORN

Native American women have been baking corn for centuries using an ancient method that adds a smoky, barbecued flavor to the natural sweetness of corn. Traditionally, they dried the corn after it was baked and used it throughout the cold, cropless winter. In busier, more modern times, baked corn is frequently frozen.

It is customary to use sweet white or yellow corn, but blue or any other color works just as well in the baking process.

The Traditional Method

Dig a large pit in the ground, approximately 3 feet deep and 4 feet wide. Line the bottom of the pit with rocks and then with dried wood. (Cottonwood is usually used because it gives off the most heat and is generously available in the Southwest.) Burn the wood until reduced to glowing embers.

Place a layer of fresh green corn husks on top of the embers, then a layer of fresh corn ears still in their husks. Top with another layer of green husks. For a pit this size about thirty ears of corn should fit. You can make the pit larger, according to how much corn you wish to bake.

Pour two buckets of water into the pit. Cover the entire pit with large burlap bags and top it with a large piece of canvas. Cover the canvas with dirt.

Allow the corn to bake overnight.

The following morning remove the corn, let cool, shuck the ears, and strip away the silk. Now it can be eaten as is, dried (by being spread outside for several days in fairly warm, dry weather), or frozen (scrape the kernels from the cob and freeze them in plastic bags).

The Modern Method

Baking corn the traditional way adds a unique flavor that cannot be duplicated by any other method of cooking. There are, however, other ways of roasting corn, and an outside barbecue grill will suffice for those who care to use an easier, less time-consuming method.

Pull back the husks from fresh corn without detaching them. Remove the silk from the corn, then smooth the husks back into place around the ears. Soak the corn for 30 minutes in enough warm water to cover.

While the corn is soaking, heat the barbecue using charcoal and mesquite wood chips. Wait until the chips become red-hot glowing embers and the coals an ashy gray color.

Drain the corn and place it on the grill for about 20 minutes. It will sizzle and spit because of the damp husks. Turn the corn every 5 minutes so that all sides are charred black.

Remove the corn from the grill and peel away the husks. The corn may be slightly charred but will have a wonderful mesquite flavor. Serve immediately, or freeze as above. (The frozen corn should keep in the freezer for several months.)

Blue Corn Dumplings in Potato Nests with Red Chile Sauce

Based on traditional ingredients, this recipe combines the mild flavors of potatoes and blue corn with the spiciness of Red Chile Sauce, resulting in a simple yet elegant appetizer.

Much of the recipe can be made a day ahead of time. The potato nests, which are made in a special pair of long-handled wire baskets, must be stored in a dry place to retain their crispness and can be served at room temperature. The chile sauce can also be made in advance, since it keeps well in the refrigerator and can easily be reheated.

POTATO BASKET

3 large Russet potatoes, peeled and julienned

4 cups vegetable oil

½ teaspoon salt

BLUE CORN DUMPLINGS

1 cup blue cornmeal

2 teaspoons baking powder

½ teaspoon salt

2 tablespoons sugar

1 teaspoon unsalted butter, melted

¾ cup milk

2 cups Chicken Stock (page 39)

1 cup water

3 cups Red Chile Sauce (page 26)

Line the larger basket in a set of long-handled potato nest baskets with potato strips and then place the smaller basket inside, on top of the potatoes.

Heat the oil in a large pot over high heat and submerge the basket in the oil. Fry about 1 minute, or until the potatoes turn golden brown. Remove the top basket and carefully remove the potato nest. Drain on paper towels. Repeat the process until you have 6 potato baskets, or until all the potato strips have been used. Sprinkle with salt and set aside.

To make the dumplings, sift the blue cornmeal, baking powder, salt, and sugar together in a bowl. Add the butter and milk and mix well, making a stiff but moist batter. Let rest 10 minutes.

Meanwhile, in a saucepan, boil together the Chicken Stock and water over high heat, then reduce the heat to a low simmer. After the batter has rested, make almond-shaped dumplings with 2 tablespoons, evening off each side of the dumpling with one of the spoons. Drop the dumplings into the simmering stock, cover the pot, and cook 3 to 4 minutes, until tender and thoroughly cooked. Drain.

Heat the Red Chile Sauce over moderate heat. Spoon about ½ cup onto each plate, place a potato basket on top and 2 to 3 dumplings inside.

Makes approximately 18 almond-shaped dumplings; serves 6 as an appetizer

BLUE CORNMEAL DUMPLINGS *are the main component of this elegant trio of appetizers.*

Red Chile Sauce

Once the summer is over, brilliant red chiles are hung in strands to dry outside many of the adobe houses in the pueblos of New Mexico and northern Arizona. Used whole or ground in many dishes, the chiles are also made into this sauce, found on the Native American table at almost all meals.

36 medium dried red anaheim chiles (about 6 cups)
3 teaspoons chopped fresh garlic
¾ teaspoon salt
3 cups Chicken Stock (page 39) or Rabbit Stock (page 130)

Rinse, stem, and seed the chiles, and place in a pot filled with water. Cover, bring to a boil over medium heat, reduce heat, and simmer 20 to 30 minutes, until tender.

Drain the cooked chiles and place them, along with the garlic and salt, in a blender or food processor. Blend to a thick puree. Add the stock and blend for another minute. Press the sauce through a fine sieve.

Makes approximately 3 cups

Squash Blossoms Stuffed with Blue Corn Dumplings in Green Chile Sauce

The Green Chile Sauce in this recipe adds just enough zest to enliven the mellow sweetness of the dumplings, creating an unusual appetizer.

18 Blue Corn Dumplings (page 25)
18 male squash blossoms (see Note)
2 cups Green Chile Sauce (page 27)

Prepare the Blue Corn Dumplings; allow to cool. Gently rinse the squash blossoms in cool water, remove the stamens, and stuff each blossom with 1 cooked dumpling. Place the blossoms in a steamer over just enough water to reach the bottom of the steamer, about 1 inch. Bring to a boil over high heat, cover, and steam the stuffed blossoms 3 minutes.

Meanwhile, heat the Green Chile Sauce. Spoon about ⅓ cup of the Green Chile Sauce onto each plate and place 3 stuffed squash blossoms on top. Serve immediately.

Serves 6 as an appetizer

NOTE: Male squash blossoms are those that do not bear fruit.

Green Chile Sauce

This sauce is an accompaniment to nearly all Native American meals.

8 green anaheim chiles
1½ cups Chicken Stock (page 39)
1 teaspoon chopped fresh garlic
¼ teaspoon salt

Using the Open-Flame Method (page 63), roast the chiles, then plunge into ice water. Stem, seed, and place chiles in a blender or food processor with the stock, garlic, and salt. Blend to a thick puree. Press through a fine sieve.

Makes approximately 2 cups

Blue Corn Dumplings with Sautéed Purslane and Squash Blossom Sauce

Purslane (or *verdolagas*) is a wild plant whose succulent, fleshy leaves are slightly tart and highly nutritious. Watercress is an acceptable substitute.

SQUASH BLOSSOM SAUCE

3 cups heavy cream
½ cup Chicken Stock (page 39)
25 squash blossoms, male or female
¼ teaspoon salt
¼ teaspoon white pepper

18 Blue Corn Dumplings (page 25)

SAUTÉED PURSLANE

1 tablespoon unsalted butter
1 teaspoon finely chopped shallots
3 cups purslane or watercress, washed and stemmed

To make the Squash Blossom Sauce, combine the cream and stock in a saucepan over medium-high heat. Simmer 5 to 10 minutes, until the mixture is reduced by half. Set aside.

Wash and stem the blossoms. If using male blossoms, remove stamens. Place the blossoms in a steamer over enough water to reach the bottom of the steamer. Bring to a boil over medium-high heat, cover, and steam blossoms 4 minutes, until tender.

Process the squash blossoms and cream mixture in a blender until smooth. Add the salt and pepper and blend 15 seconds. Press through a fine sieve to remove any pulp. Gently reheat the sauce and keep warm over low heat until ready to serve.

Prepare the Blue Corn Dumplings. While they are cooking, melt the butter in a saucepan over medium heat, add the shallots, and sauté until translucent, stirring occasionally. Add purslane and stir until warm but not limp.

When the dumplings are cooked, remove from the heat and drain.

Spoon some of the Squash Blossom Sauce onto each plate and top with 3 dumplings and some of the purslane greens. Serve immediately.

Serves 6 as an appetizer

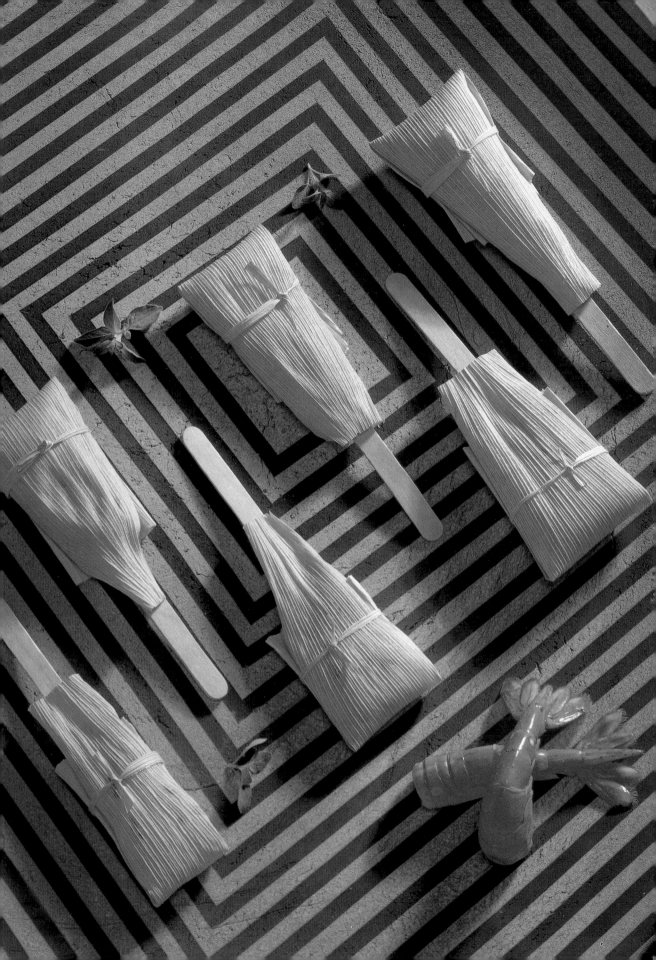

The unusual presentation makes the CORNSICLES *(left) special, and* ARROWHEADS OF BLUE CORNMEAL GNOCCHI *(above) put a Southwest twist on an Italian classic.*

Cornsicles with Shrimp and Oregano

Traditionally, this recipe is made with blue corn alone; the sweet, fresh taste needs no embellishment. However, to enhance the flavor of commercial sweet yellow corn, I have added shrimp and oregano, resulting in a wonderful appetizer or accompaniment.

6 ears corn

1 teaspoon salt

¼ teaspoon white pepper

1 tablespoon chopped fresh oregano, or 1 teaspoon dried

12 medium shrimp, peeled, deveined, and diced

24 popsicle sticks

Trim the corn and remove the husks and silk. Save and wash the larger husks. Cut the corn kernels from the cob, scraping out as much milk as you can.

Grind the kernels using a meat grinder with a sharp blade. (A food processor can be used, but be sure to stir the corn well before continuing.) Add the salt, white pepper, oregano, and shrimp and mix well.

Preheat the oven to 325° F.

Drop a tablespoon of the corn mixture onto the center of a clean husk. Fold the left side of the husk into the center, then the right, and then fold the bottom end upward. Push a popsicle stick 2 to 3 inches into the open end and pinch the husk around the stick with your fingers. Tear a thin strand from a dry husk and tie it around the cornsicle.

Place the rolls, sticks in the air and very close together, in a glass baking dish or loaf pan. Bake 30 minutes, until the corn mixture is firm and solid.

To eat a cornsicle, peel off the corn husk and eat it hot from the stick, as you would a popsicle.

Makes about 2 dozen; serves 6 as an appetizer

Arrowheads of Blue Corn Gnocchi with Guajillo Chile Sauce

In this dish I have used blue cornmeal, a basic ingredient in Native American southwest cooking, to make gnocchi, a classic Italian potato dumpling. The cornmeal makes the dough thicker and more pliable, which makes cutting the dumplings into interesting shapes for presentation very easy.

BLUE CORN GNOCCHI

2 medium Russet potatoes

8 quarts water

5 ounces (approximately ½ cup) soft white goat cheese

4 eggs

1½ cups all-purpose flour

1½ cups blue cornmeal

2 tablespoons salt

GUAJILLO CHILE SAUCE
**3 ounces dried red guajillo chiles (about 15
chiles, or 2¼ cups)**
½ cup dried pumpkin seeds
½ teaspoon salt
½ teaspoon white pepper
5½ cups water

To make the gnocchi, peel and boil the potatoes in 2 quarts water until soft and cooked through.

In a food processor, combine the potatoes and goat cheese and process until lump free, about 2 minutes. Add the eggs and process another minute. The mixture should resemble putty.

Stir the flour and blue cornmeal together. Pour the potato mixture into a bowl and add 2 cups of the flour-cornmeal mixture. Mix together thoroughly to form the dough.

Dust a wooden cutting board with half the remaining flour-cornmeal mixture and place the dough on top. Flatten it and sprinkle it with the remaining flour and cornmeal. Knead the flour and cornmeal into the dough until it becomes stiff. The dough is ready when it no longer clings to the board. If the mixture is still soft, damp, and sticky, add a little more flour.

With your hands, shape the dough on a board into a long roll 2 inches in diameter. With a knife cut the dough into slices 1 inch thick.

Flour another board and roll each 1-inch piece into a thin strip about ½-inch wide and 16 inches long. Flatten the strips, with your hands, to about 1 inch wide, and cut the dough with a knife into arrowheads, or any other shapes you desire. Set aside.

To make the Guajillo Chile Sauce, put the chiles, pumpkin seeds, salt, and pepper in a food processor and process for 1 minute. Add the water, in small amounts, until completely blended, about 4 minutes. Press the mixture through a fine sieve and discard the pulp.

In a saucepan, heat the chile mixture over medium-high heat 4 minutes, until it begins to boil. Reduce the heat and simmer 15 minutes, until thickened.

While the sauce is simmering, cook the gnocchi. In a large pot, bring the 6 quarts water to a boil with the salt. Add the gnocchi and cook 2 to 3 minutes (see Note), gently stirring frequently so that they don't stick. At first the gnocchi will sink to the bottom; as they cook, they will begin to hold their shape and float to the surface.

Once the gnocchi have risen to the top, remove them from the boiling water with a slotted spoon.

Spoon ½ cup sauce on each plate, top with the gnocchi, and serve immediately.

Serves 6 as an appetizer

NOTE: At higher altitudes, gnocchi can take longer to cook. Test before serving.

Hopi dishes like PIKI *(left) and* SOMEVIKI *(above) are made from cornmeal ground with a stone matate and grinding stone, shown in both pictures.*

Traditional Yellow *Piki* Bread with Spinach Greens in *Tuitsma* Sauce

This light, colorful appetizer combines *Piki* Bread made from yellow cornmeal with lightly cooked spinach. *Tuitsma* is the Indian name for cinchweed, an herb that grows wild in northern Arizona. Its closest common relative is lemon thyme.

4 tablespoons (½ stick) unsalted butter
2 tablespoons dried *tuitsma* flowers, or
   1 tablespoon dried lemon thyme
½ teaspoon salt
½ teaspoon black pepper
2 cups Veal Stock (page 38)
1 bunch (about 4 cups, lightly packed) large
   spinach leaves, thoroughly washed, stemmed,
   and drained
6 yellow cornmeal *Piki* Breads (page 148)

In a saucepan over moderate heat, melt the butter. Add 1 tablespoon of the *tuitsma* (or ½ tablespoon lemon thyme), salt, and pepper; cook 2 minutes. Add the stock and simmer briskly until it is reduced by half.

Stir in the spinach leaves and simmer 1 minute more. Spoon the spinach and sauce onto large serving plates. Place a *Piki* Bread on top of each plate. Garnish with the remaining *tuitsma* or lemon thyme.

Serves 6 as an appetizer

Traditional Blue Corn *Piki* Bread with Scallops and Shrimp in *Azafrán* Sauce

Blue corn varies in color from bluish gray to almost black and is still an important crop to the Hopis today.

4 tablespoons (½ stick) unsalted butter
½ cup Fish Stock (page 39)
2 tablespoons *azafrán* (Native American saffron;
   see Note, page 83)
1 cup heavy cream
12 bay scallops
12 medium shrimp, peeled and deveined, tails
   left on
6 blue cornmeal *Piki* Breads (page 148)

Melt the butter in a saucepan over moderate heat. Add the fish stock and bring to a boil. Add 1 tablespoon of the *azafrán* and reduce the heat. Simmer 3 minutes, then slowly stir in the cream. Simmer until thick and reduced by about one third.

Add the scallops to the sauce and simmer over medium heat 2 minutes. Add the shrimp and simmer 2 minutes more, until the shrimp are cooked.

Pour some of the sauce across the middle of each of 6 large heated serving plates. Place a *Piki* Bread on top, with shrimp and scallops on either side. Garnish with the remaining *azafrán*.

Serves 6 as an appetizer

Someviki with Red Chile Sauce

Someviki are sweet blue cornmeal dumplings similar to the blue corn dumplings on page 25. They are wrapped in corn husks, tied, and boiled until cooked.

30 dried corn husks
5 tablespoons culinary ash (see Note, page 21)
   or 2 teaspoons baking soda
2 cups boiling water
2 cups finely ground blue cornmeal
½ cup sugar
Red Chile Sauce (page 26)

Soak the corn husks in very hot water for 10 to 15 minutes until they are soft and pliable.

Mix the culinary ash with ½ cup of the boiling water and set aside.

Mix the blue cornmeal and sugar together in a bowl. Add the remaining boiling water and stir until the mixture is thick.

Pour the ash-water through a fine strainer; discard ash. Add the ash-water to the cornmeal mixture, small amounts at a time, while stirring to make the dough. It will turn a distinctive blue color and should have the consistency of a thick cake batter.

Spoon 1 tablespoon of the dough onto each corn husk and fold the husk around the dough, first the sides and then the ends. Tear long, thin strands from another husk and tie each bundle to secure the dough inside. (If you find the corn-husk strands too difficult to manipulate, use string instead.)

Bring a large pot of water to a boil, drop the wrapped husks into the water, and simmer 10 minutes. Once the husks have plumped, remove them from the water and drain. Serve with Red Chile Sauce. Untie the corn husks after serving so that the dumplings stay hot.

Makes 30 someviki; *serves 10 as an appetizer*

HAZRUQUIVE is traditionally served on the day of the Bean Dance, when prayers are made to the kachinas, which may be represented by figures such as the doll at upper right.

Hazruquive
(HOMINY, BEAN SPROUT, AND CORNCOB STEW)

This recipe is based on a traditional Hopi dish made once a year, on the day of the Powanu Ceremony, or Bean Dance, in late winter when the land is in the period of its deepest dormancy. It is on this day that the Kachinas carry a basket full of bean sprouts that have somehow grown during the dark, cold days of winter.

The Bean Dance is a formal prayer to the Kachinas on behalf of the seeds that will be planted as soon as the frozen ground thaws and spring, which signifies life, arrives.

I have adapted this recipe for the modern kitchen using fresh corn because dried corn on the cob is not readily available commercially; however, the essence of the dish remains traditional.

2 cups cooked Indian Hominy (page 22)
3 cups Veal Stock (page 38)
1 tablespoon salt
1 teaspoon black pepper
3 ears yellow corn on the cob, cut into 3- to
    4-inch pieces
2 bunches bean or sunflower sprouts

Place the hominy in a large sauce-pan with enough water to cover. Bring to a boil over high heat and add the Veal Stock, salt, and pepper. Return to a boil, reduce the heat to medium, and cook 10 minutes.

Add the corn and continue cooking 10 minutes longer, or until the corn is tender.

Add the bean sprouts, reduce the heat to low, and simmer until they also are tender, 5 to 10 minutes.

Serve hot. Customarily the corn is eaten with the hands, and the hominy and broth are eaten with a spoon. *Hazruquive* tastes wonderful with *Piki* Bread (page 148) or other breads.

Serves 6

Veal Stock

The flavor of veal stock is unlike that of any other stock; it has a distinctively delicious taste. I strongly advise you to use veal stock when it is suggested in a recipe. The loin bones and knuckles can be purchased at your local butcher; usually they are available in the early morning. Be sure to ask for bones with the marrow, which contains most of the flavor.

5 pounds veal bones (loin or knuckle)
1 tablespoon olive oil
5 ripe tomatoes, quartered
2 leeks, coarsely chopped
5 celery stalks, coarsely chopped
4 large carrots, coarsely chopped
6 quarts water
4 bay leaves
1 bunch fresh parsley
2 bunches fresh thyme

Preheat the oven to 450° F. Put bones in a large roasting pan and brown in the oven about 1 hour, turning them every 20 minutes. Remove from the oven and set aside.

In a large stock pot combine the olive oil, tomatoes, leeks, celery, and carrots and sauté over high heat for 15 minutes, stirring constantly.

Add the bones, water, and herbs and bring to a boil over medium heat. Reduce heat and simmer for 4½ to 5 hours, skimming the surface every half hour until all remnants of fat and foam disappear. Remove from heat and carefully strain the stock through a sieve lined with cheesecloth. Discard the contents of the sieve.

Refrigerate stock 3 hours, then remove solidified fat from the top. The stock will keep 5 days in a covered container.

Although better fresh, the stock can also be frozen in ice cube trays; the cubes can be stored in plastic bags in the freezer for several months. Larger quantities of stock can be poured directly into plastic bags and stored in the freezer.

Makes 4 quarts

Fish Stock

4 to 6 pounds halibut or white fish bones, with heads and tails
3 carrots, coarsely chopped
2 celery stalks, coarsely chopped
2 large onions, quartered
2 bay leaves
1 bunch fresh parsley
1 tablespoon black peppercorns
5 quarts water

Rinse the fish bones under cold running water and remove the gills.

In a large stockpot combine the fish bones, carrots, celery, onions, bay leaves, parsley, peppercorns, and water and bring to a boil over high heat. Reduce the heat and simmer 45 minutes, until the stock is reduced by half. Skim the top frequently to remove foam.

Remove from the heat and pour through a fine sieve lined with cheesecloth; discard solids. Let cool. Pour into a container and place in the refrigerator. The stock will keep 5 days in a covered container.

The stock can also be frozen and will last up to several months in the freezer, although it does taste best fresh. Freeze in ice cube trays and then store the cubes in the freezer in plastic bags. Larger quantities of stock can be poured directly into plastic bags and stored in the freezer.

Makes 2½ quarts

Chicken Stock

2 large chicken carcasses
4 celery stalks, coarsely chopped
4 large carrots, coarsely chopped
2 large leeks, coarsely chopped
2 medium yellow onions, quartered
1 bunch fresh parsley
3 bay leaves
1 bunch fresh thyme
8 quarts water

Combine all the ingredients in a large stockpot and bring to a boil over medium heat. Reduce heat to low and simmer about 1 hour, skimming off the fat as it rises to the surface. Continue simmering over low heat until the stock has been reduced by one third and the flavor has intensified.

Remove from the heat and carefully strain the stock through a sieve lined with cheesecloth. Discard the contents of the sieve. Pour the stock into a container and let cool. Then place the stock in the refrigerator for 3 hours. Remove solidified fat from the top. The stock will keep 5 days in a covered container.

Although Chicken Stock tastes better fresh, it can also be frozen in ice cube trays; store the cubes in plastic bags in the freezer up to 2 months. Larger quantities of stock can be poured directly into plastic bags and stored in the freezer.

Makes about 5 quarts

The sauces decorating **PIÑON AND BLUE CORNMEAL HOTCAKES** *(above) echo patterns in the blanket and basket. Three colors are featured in* **CORN AND HONEY PASTEL ICE** *(right).*

Piñon and Blue Cornmeal Hotcakes with Prickly Pear Syrup and Peach Honey

Native American women used to make hotcakes with only blue cornmeal flour, goat's milk, cedar ash, and water, but today most of them make the dish as follows.

PIÑON HOTCAKES

1½ cups shelled piñons (pine nuts)
1 cup all-purpose flour
½ teaspoon salt
2 tablespoons sugar
1 cup milk

BLUE CORNMEAL HOTCAKES

1½ cups blue cornmeal
2 tablespoons sugar
1 tablespoon baking powder
1 teaspoon salt
3 tablespoons unsalted butter, melted
2 eggs, beaten
1 cup milk

4 tablespoons (½ stick) unsalted butter, melted, for greasing griddle

Prickly Pear Syrup (recipe follows)
Peach Honey (page 43)

For the Piñon Hotcakes, grind the piñons to a coarse meal in a blender. Mix the ground nut meal together with the flour, salt, and sugar, and add the milk to form a stiff batter. Set aside and let stand 1 hour before cooking.

In a large bowl, combine the cornmeal, sugar, baking powder, and salt for the Blue Cornmeal Hotcakes. Add the butter, then the eggs and milk, mixing thoroughly.

Warm a griddle over medium heat and lightly brush with the butter.

Drop spoonfuls of the batters onto the griddle. The Piñon Hotcakes may have to be pressed with a well-greased spatula into ¼- to ½-inch-thick cakes, 3 inches in diameter, because the batter is very thick. Turn the cakes once as they begin to brown. To keep the finished hotcakes warm, stack them on a cookie sheet, cover them with a clean towel, and place them in the oven set at a very low heat. Butter the griddle between each batch.

Serve with the Prickly Pear Syrup and Peach Honey.

Makes 35 to 40 hotcakes; serves 6

Prickly Pear Syrup

Prickly pears have a sweet, tangy flavor that makes a delicious syrup, excellent with the Piñon and Blue Cornmeal Hotcakes (page 42) and also a wonderful topping for the Corn and Honey Pastel Ice (page 43) or Picuris Indian Bread Pudding (page 150).

12 prickly pears (page 79)
¼ cup honey

Wash and cut each prickly pear

into quarters, leaving the skins on.

Place the fruit in a food processor and process until pulpy and thoroughly blended. Press the liquid through a fine sieve; discard skin and seeds.

Put the prickly pear juice into a saucepan with the honey and bring to a boil over medium-high heat. Reduce the heat and let simmer 10 minutes, until the mixture has thickened. Remove from the heat and let cool. The syrup will thicken further as it cools. The syrup may be stored in the refrigerator for up to 1 week.

Makes approximately 1 cup

Peach Honey

Peach Honey can accompany a variety of dishes. I use it with the Piñon and Blue Cornmeal Hotcakes (page 42), Feast Days Piñon Torte (page 106), and Adobe Bread (page 146).

1 pound fresh peaches, peeled, pitted, and
**   sliced, or dried peaches (see Note)**
3 tablespoons honey
1 teaspoon freshly squeezed lemon juice

Blend all ingredients together in a food processor for 3 minutes to make a smooth puree. Pour into a squeeze bottle.

Peach Honey can be kept in the refrigerator for 1 to 2 weeks.

Makes 1 cup

NOTE: If using dried peaches, soak them in water to cover for 1½ hours, until soft and pliable. Remove the skins with your fingers, then proceed with the recipe, adding an extra tablespoon of honey, if necessary, to compensate for the tartness of the dried fruit.

Corn and Honey Pastel Ice

Southwest Indians achieve pastel colors by using dried red or blue corn. You can use fresh white corn and add 2 tablespoons blue cornmeal to the saucepan for a blue ice, or a few fresh raspberries or strawberries for red.

3 cups fresh corn kernels
1 tablespoon vegetable oil
1 cup water
⅓ cup honey

Place the corn and oil in a saucepan and cook over medium heat 4 minutes, stirring constantly to prevent the corn from browning. Transfer the corn to a blender and add the water and honey. Blend until very smooth.

Return the mixture to the saucepan and bring it to a boil. Reduce the heat and simmer, uncovered, stirring frequently, about 15 minutes, until it has a thick, porridgelike consistency.

Freeze for at least 6 hours or place in an ice cream maker and follow the manufacturer's directions.

Serves 6

GROWN FROM THE VINE

CHILES, TOMATOES, SQUASH, AND MELONS

The Native Americans of the Southwest are known for their expertise in the farming and harvesting of many different foods. They have a particular talent for the propagation of vine-grown fruits and vegetables, some of which, such as squash, are indigenous to North America while others, such as chiles, tomatoes, and melons, were brought north from South America by migrating tribes thousands of years ago.

Most vine-grown fruits and squash are harvested in late summer and throughout the fall. When harvest season arrives and there is an abundance of chiles or squash and even melons and tomatoes, they are roasted and dried, or simply dried in the hot desert sun, and stored away for later use. And with modern conveniences such as freezers, produce can be frozen and kept for months.

The most popular of these vine-grown fruits is the chile, the powerful essence of southwestern cooking. Chiles are believed to have come from the Mayans and Aztecs, the Indians of Mexico. They were traded with other tribes, the Papagos and Pimas, and other varieties were created and slowly brought north. Chiles are the main ingredient of numerous recipes and are a pleasantly pungent addition to others. There are various types of chiles that range in size, color, flavor, and degree of hotness and each is used differently.

Squash has been an important part of the Native American diet for thousands of years. Squash blossoms are considered a delicacy, especially among the Zuni tribe. If picked in the early morning before the flowers open up to the sun, they can be fried, blanched, or stuffed, adding an exotic touch to many dishes. Recently more popular, squash blossoms can now be found in specialty markets; they do not keep well and should be eaten the day you buy or pick them. For winter use, the seeds are removed from the squash and the flesh is cut into strips and dried in the sun.

Pumpkins, America's favorite squash, also produce edible blossoms; roasted pumpkin seeds make a healthy snack. The light, spicy flesh of the pumpkin can be used in dishes from soup to cookies.

Melon, also grown from the vine, has always been enjoyed as a refresher in hot weather, and is also dried in the desert sun in long, spiral strips and stored for later use. Dried melon is eaten as a snack throughout the winter and is also stewed with honey or sugar and used in desserts.

Tomatoes, fresh and plump, taste especially sweet in the summer. They are most famously used in the Southwest for salsas; varying degrees of hotness come from the addition of chiles. The tomatillo is a small tart green fruit similar in appearance to the completely unrelated common tomato, but with a leaflike husk. Native to Mexico, the tomatillo grows abundantly in the wild and was brought north by migrating tribes.

All of these wonderful vine-grown fruits and vegetables have been cultivated for centuries in the Southwest and have provided sustenance for many tribes. Nowadays, the same produce is widely available in markets throughout the country, inspiring a renewed appreciation of many traditional Native American dishes.

Variations of RIO GRANDE PIZZAS *(left),*
and FRESH GREEN CHILE SOUP.

Indian Salsa

Almost every pueblo and tribe I visited on my travels throughout the Southwest had its own recipe for salsa, which is used as a condiment for every meal. All the salsas I tasted were hot and spicy to my palate; this recipe is a combination of the many I tried. If you find it too hot for your taste, cut the amount of jalapeños in half.

11 tomatillos, husked and finely chopped
4 large ripe tomatoes, finely chopped

¾ cup finely chopped onion
3 garlic cloves, finely chopped
**6 jalapeño peppers, seeded, deveined
 and finely chopped**
½ cup finely chopped fresh cilantro
1 teaspoon freshly squeezed lime juice

Toss together all the ingredients in a bowl. Allow to marinate about 1 hour to bring out the full flavor. Serve cold or at room temperature.

Makes approximately 4 cups

Rio Grande Pizzas

The following pizza recipe was inspired by the abundance of produce that is available in the Southwest during the summer months. Red, ripe tomatoes are sweet and delicate in flavor; chiles range in taste from subtle to robust; and fresh herbs are pungent and aromatic. These ingredients provide a vigorous and distinctive flavor.

4 green anaheim chiles
1½ cups Fresh Tomato Sauce (recipe follows)
6 Blue Cornmeal Tortillas (page 141), baked
5 ounces (approximately ½ cup) soft white goat cheese
1 bunch chives, chopped
6 strips thinly sliced Garlic Jerky (see Variation, page 135)
2 tablespoons chopped fresh basil leaves

Roast the chiles by the Oven or Open-Flame methods (pages 62–63), then peel, seed, devein, and chop them. Preheat the oven to 400° F.

Heat the tomato sauce in a saucepan over medium heat. Spoon approximately ¼ cup sauce over each tortilla and crumble the goat cheese, green chiles, chives, and Garlic Jerky on top.

Place the pizzas on a baking sheet and cook in the oven 7 to 10 minutes, until the cheese is melted and the pizzas are hot. Sprinkle the fresh basil on top and serve immediately.

Serves 6

VARIATIONS:

This master pizza recipe can be varied according to what you find in the garden, the market, and your imagination. Grilled rabbit, beans, tomatillos, and raw onions are all successful additions.

Fresh Tomato Sauce

Unlike many tomato sauces, this one is rich and thick and works well as a base for many recipes in addition to the pizzas.

24 fresh tomatoes, peeled, seeded, and quartered
1 small onion, diced
2 garlic cloves, finely chopped
2 tablespoons olive oil
½ teaspoon salt
½ teaspoon white pepper
1 bay leaf
1 tablespoon finely chopped fresh basil leaves
2 teaspoons finely chopped fresh oregano leaves

Puree the tomatoes in a food processor until smooth, approximately 1 minute.

In a large saucepan over medium heat, sauté the onion and garlic in the olive oil until the onions are translucent. Add the tomato puree, salt, pepper, bay leaf, basil, and oregano and mix together. Lower the heat and simmer approximately 1 hour until the sauce is reduced by half and becomes a thicker paste.

Makes approximately 2 cups

Fresh Green Chile Soup with Tumbleweed Greens

Green chiles are commonly found in most southwestern kitchens. They are used as a condiment by Native Americans in northern Arizona and throughout the pueblos of New Mexico. Here they are used as a base for a spicy soup. The garnish of tumbleweed greens and sour cream is a refreshingly cool contrast to the fiery taste of the chiles.

This dish can be served as a meal in itself with Indian Frybread (page 150), *Piki* Bread (page 148), or Adobe Bread (page 146). It also makes an excellent first course.

12 green anaheim chiles
2 medium red bell peppers
2 very large Russet potatoes, peeled and cut
    into ½-inch cubes
2½ teaspoons salt
6 cups Chicken Stock (page 39)
1 teaspoon black pepper
3 garlic cloves, chopped
6 tablespoons sour cream, for garnish
¼ cup tumbleweed greens, for garnish

Roast the chiles and peppers by the Open-Flame Method (page 63). Peel the chiles and peppers, pull off the stems, remove the seeds and veins, and set aside.

In a medium saucepan, parboil the potatoes in boiling water with 1 teaspoon of the salt until tender.

Puree the green chiles and then the red peppers separately in a food processor until smooth. Mix the purees together, add the potatoes and stock, and process in 2-cup batches for another minute, or until smooth. Add the remaining salt, the pepper, and garlic and process again. Press the puree through a fine sieve.

Heat the puree in a saucepan. Serve hot, garnished with sour cream and the tumbleweed greens.

Serves 6

Just-picked chiles add zest to the **FRESH CHILE AND CORN FRITTERS.**

PUMPKIN CORN SOUP *is filled with the bounty of the fall harvest.*

Fresh Chile and Corn Fritters with Julienne of Tart Indian Apples

Although Native Americans dry many foods for use throughout the year, they always prefer the fresh taste of foods recently harvested: the corn is sweeter, the chiles spicier, and the

apples are tart. During the late summer, when these fruits and vegetables are harvested in the northern parts of Arizona and New Mexico, a dish such as this, which combines an array of different flavors, is a fall favorite.

CHILE AND CORN FRITTERS

4 green anaheim chiles
3 cups corn kernels, scraped from the cob
3 green serrano chiles, seeded and chopped
1 teaspoon salt
½ teaspoon white pepper
3 tablespoons all-purpose flour
¾ cup clarified butter (see Note)

JULIENNE OF APPLES

1 tablespoon unsalted butter
6 small green apples, cored and julienned
  (do not peel)
½ teaspoon celery seed

Roast the anaheim chiles (see pages 62–63), then peel, seed, and dice them.

Process the corn in a food processor until it resembles a puree, about 2 minutes. Scrape down with a spatula and process for another minute.

In a bowl, mix together the corn puree, the chopped chiles, salt, and pepper. Slowly add the flour, small amounts at a time, while stirring.

In a medium saucepan, heat the clarified butter over high heat. Using a large cook's spoon or serving spoon, gently drop spoonfuls of the batter into the hot butter. When the edges are brown after about 2 minutes, turn the fritters over and cook another 2 min-

utes. Remove the fritters and allow them to drain on paper towels.

In another saucepan over medium-high heat, melt the unsalted butter, add the apples and the celery seed, and sauté about 3 minutes, until they begin to soften. Serve hot with the fritters.

Makes 12 to 15 fritters

NOTE: To make clarified butter, melt butter over low heat, then set aside to cool. When the milk solids have separated from the liquid, skim the top layer of froth from the butter with a spoon and discard. Pour off the clarified butter, discarding the residue on the bottom.

Pumpkin Corn Soup with Ginger Lime Cream

This simple recipe is easy to prepare and utilizes two very basic ingredients in southwestern cooking: pumpkin and corn. It is a delicious, rich-bodied soup, and the Ginger Lime Cream adds a refreshing zest.

PUMPKIN CORN SOUP

3 cups corn kernels
2 garlic cloves, finely chopped
¾ teaspoon salt
¾ teaspoon white pepper
3 cups Chicken Stock (page 39)
3 cups Cooked Pumpkin (page 55)

GINGER LIME CREAM
Juice and zest of 2 limes
1 tablespoon peeled and grated fresh ginger
½ cup heavy cream

In a medium covered pot, cook the corn kernels with a little water until soft, about 10 minutes. In a food processor, process the corn until smooth, about 2 minutes. Run through a sieve and discard the skins.

Combine the corn puree, garlic, salt, white pepper, and stock in a saucepan and bring to a boil over medium-high heat. Reduce the heat to low, add the pumpkin, and cook 10 minutes while stirring.

In another saucepan cook the lime juice and ginger 2 minutes over medium heat. Remove from the heat and pour through a sieve to remove the ginger.

In a bowl, combine the ginger-lime juice, the lime zest (save some for the garnish), and cream. Whip until the mixture has soft peaks.

Spoon a dollop of Ginger Lime Cream onto each bowl filled with soup and garnish with the remaining lime zest. Serve immediately.

Serves 6

Cooked Pumpkin

Pumpkin is a winter squash that has been cultivated for hundreds of years in the Southwest. It ranges in size from several inches to several feet and can be round or oblong in shape. The average cooking pumpkin is usually between 10 and 25 pounds. The meat, the seeds, and the pumpkin's blossoms are all edible and can be prepared in many different ways. Pumpkin pulp is also sold in 16-ounce cans, which makes a convenient substitute for fresh cooked pumpkin in recipes.

Fresh pumpkin, however, always tastes better. Here is the method I use to cook it: Cut the pumpkin into quarters and remove the seeds and fibers. Preheat the oven to 350° F. and bake the pumpkin quarters 45 minutes, until tender. Remove from the oven and scrape the flesh from the skin. Place in a food processor and purée. Run through a sieve to remove any remaining fibers and use the pumpkin according to recipe instructions.

Cooked pumpkin will keep about 1 week in a nonmetal, covered container in the refrigerator and several months in the freezer.

Two pounds of fresh pumpkin—skin, seeds, and fiber removed—makes approximately 2 cups of cooked pumpkin

FRIED SQUASH BLOSSOMS *are served with celery sauce (left).*
SQUASH BLOSSOM SOUP *(above) has an unusual flavor.*

Fried Squash Blossoms with Celery Sauce

Squash blossoms, considered by the Zuni tribe in western New Mexico to be great delicacies, are eaten and enjoyed in many of the pueblos along the Rio Grande. The flowers are carefully gathered in the early morning before the blossoms open up to the sun. Male blossoms are gathered because they do not bear fruit and are larger than the female blossoms —

and better able to hold their form when used in cooking. There are several commercial growers willing to ship the male blossoms to the consumer, but the female blossoms that are attached to the baby squash found in specialty markets can also be used.

FRIED SQUASH BLOSSOMS

1 green anaheim chile
½ cup water
1 egg, beaten
1 cup all-purpose flour
½ cup heavy cream
1 tablespoon unsalted butter
1 onion, finely chopped
2 tomatoes, peeled, seeded, and coarsely chopped
1 garlic clove, finely chopped
½ teaspoon salt
¼ teaspoon white pepper

30 squash blossoms, preferably male
2 to 3 cups vegetable oil

CELERY SAUCE

1 pound celery, leaves and stalks
3 tablespoons unsalted butter
½ teaspoon salt

Roast, peel, seed (see pages 62–63), and dice the anaheim chile.

In a bowl mix together the water, egg, flour, and cream to make the batter and set aside 1 hour.

Melt the butter in a saucepan over medium-low heat and sauté the onion until it is translucent. Add the tomatoes, chile, garlic, salt, and pepper, re-duce heat to low, and simmer 15 minutes. Stir occasionally to prevent burning. Remove from the heat and let cool.

To make the sauce, cut the celery into large chunks and place in a pot with enough salted water to cover. Bring to a boil over high heat and cook about 20 minutes until celery is tender.

Drain the water, place the celery in a food processor, and purée. Strain through a fine sieve into a saucepan.

Heat the celery puree over medium-low heat 8 to 10 minutes, until reduced by half. Add the butter and salt and stir together until the sauce is smooth and shiny. Keep warm until the squash blossoms are fried.

Remove stamens from male squash blossoms. Fill each blossom with about 1 tablespoon of the sautéed vegetables and spices, pull together the tip of the blossom to seal in the filling, and gently dip it into the batter, covering the entire blossom.

Heat the oil in a large saucepan or fryer until it is very hot but not smoking. Gently drop each blossom into the oil. Fry 3 to 5 minutes, turning once, until the blossoms are golden brown. Remove the blossoms with a slotted spoon and drain on paper towels.

Using a sharp knife, slice each blossom twice diagonally. Spoon about ¼ cup sauce onto each of 6 plates, top with the fried squash blossoms, and serve hot.

Serves 6 as an appetizer

NOTE: You can vary this recipe by inserting a scant teaspoonful of goat cheese into the blossom before stuffing.

Squash Blossom Soup

This light, clear soup has a subtle, flowery taste that is quite unusual. Serve it in the summer when squash blossoms are readily available. Plan to use squash blossoms the day you purchase or pick them, as they tend to wilt easily and lose their delicate form and flavor.

60 squash blossoms, washed
1 tablespoon unsalted butter
½ cup chopped wild onions (see Note) or yellow onions
2 garlic cloves, finely chopped
1 teaspoon salt
½ teaspoon white pepper
6 cups Chicken Stock (page 39)
18 sprigs fresh chervil for garnish

If using male squash blossoms, remove the stamens. Set aside.

Melt the butter in a saucepan over medium heat. Add the onions and garlic and sauté until the onions are translucent. Reduce the heat to low, add the salt, pepper, and squash blossoms and sauté 3 minutes, stirring occasionally to prevent burning. Add the stock, bring to a boil over high heat, reduce the heat to low, and simmer 10 minutes. Remove from the heat and serve hot, garnished with sprigs of chervil.

Serves 6

NOTE: The wild onion grows throughout the Southwest during the spring and summer. It thrives best in moist soil and can be found at an elevation anywhere from 1,000 to 10,000 feet. It grows from a basal bulb, the part of the wild onion that can be used like a regular onion in cooking and sautéing. The leaf of the wild onion is long and tubular, resembling a scallion or chive; it can be chopped and used similarly. The wild onion also has flowers ranging in color from white to pale pink, which are edible and make an attractive garnish.

Mesa Squash Fry with Sunflower Seeds

This colorful squash fry is a favorite dish enjoyed at harvest time.

1 green anaheim chile
1 tablespoon sunflower oil
2 garlic cloves, finely chopped
½ teaspoon salt
½ teaspoon black pepper
8 ears sweet yellow corn, kernels cut from the cob
8 small zucchini or yellow squash, cut into 2-inch-long julienne
1 red bell pepper, diced
¼ cup shelled sunflower seeds

Roast the anaheim chile (see pages 62–63), then peel, seed, and coarsely chop it.

In a sauté pan, heat the oil over moderate heat. When the oil is hot but not smoking add the garlic, chile, salt, and pepper and cook 1 to 2 minutes, stirring constantly, to allow the flavors to blend.

Add the corn, squash, and red pepper. Reduce heat and allow the vegetables to simmer about 15 minutes, until they are tender.

Add the sunflower seeds and simmer another 5 minutes. Serve hot as a vegetable side dish.

Serves 6

Chile Pepper Jelly

Chile Pepper Jelly is one way of preserving chiles — and it makes a delicious condiment at any meal.

1 tablespoon chopped serrano chiles
1 cup diced anaheim chiles
1 medium green bell pepper, diced
1¼ cups red wine vinegar
5 cups sugar
6 ounces liquid pectin or 1 package (1¾ ounces) powdered pectin

Combine the chiles and pepper with the vinegar in a food processor. Process 3 minutes until puréed.

Put the puree and sugar in a saucepan. Bring the mixture to a hard rolling boil over medium-high heat, stirring constantly. Remove from the heat, skim the foam from the top, discard, and add the pectin. Return to the heat and bring again to a hard boil for 2 minutes, stirring constantly. Remove from the heat and stir constantly 5 minutes.

As it cools the jelly will begin to thicken. Pour it into clean, sterilized 8-ounce jars, leaving a ¼-inch space at the top. Seal as desired.

Makes 6 8-ounce jars

MESA SQUASH FRY *presents a colorful contrast to its copper patina background.*

CHOOSING AND COOKING WITH CHILES

There are many types of chiles, ranging from mild to fiery hot. The degree of heat depends on the time of harvest — red chiles are riper, of course, and taste sweeter and somewhat hotter than green — and also on the variety and the growing and handling techniques used.

The most commonly used chile is the *anaheim*. It is fairly large — 6 to 7 inches long — with mild heat. Harvested green, it is a favorite for stuffing or for roasting and using in sauces and stews. When harvested red, the anaheim is strung in *ristras*, large strands of chiles that are hung outside in the sun to dry. It can then be ground into chile powder.

The *New Mexico green* chile is similar to the anaheim, and the two are interchangeable in my recipes. The New Mexico green is slightly smaller than the anaheim, and varies in strength from medium to very hot, depending on the region it was grown in. The *New Mexico red* is a ripened New Mexico green. It can be used fresh or frozen, but it is more commonly dried and powdered.

The *jalapeño*, about 3 inches long, has a fiery hot taste and, although usually eaten green, can also be matured on the vine and ripened to red. It is added raw to salsas and salads or cooked in sauces, soups, and stews. Jalapeños are roasted, then dried.

The *serrano*, a smaller chile, can be substituted for the jalapeño. It has a hot but fruity flavor when eaten green; the red pods can be dried but taste best eaten fresh.

The fresh *cayenne* pepper is about 4 to 7 inches in length, and ¼ to ¾ inch wide. It is a hot, sweet chile with thin flesh that tends to twist as it grows; it has the best flavor when it is red and mature, but is also eaten green.

The *Holland* chile is a hybrid that is available all year and tastes very similar to a fresh cayenne pepper.

The *guajillo* is a tough-skinned dried brownish-red chile about 4 inches in length. It has a rich, earthy flavor that is fruity with a medium hotness.

Other extremely hot chiles that are eaten dried include the *chile de árbol* and the *chile pequín*. Both should be used sparingly.

Handling Chiles

Always wash fresh and dried chiles to remove dirt. Whenever handling chiles, always take precautions to avoid skin irritation: wear rubber gloves and *do not* rub your eyes.

Roasting Chiles

There are various techniques for roasting chiles, each resulting in a slightly different flavor. Red and yellow bell peppers can be roasted by the same methods.

The Oven Method

Preheat the oven to 450° F., place the chiles on a baking sheet, and bake 20 to 30 minutes. Turn the chiles frequently as they begin to brown until all sides are evenly blistered and browned. Remove from the oven.

"Sweat" the chiles in a closed paper or plastic bag 5 to 10 minutes until they are cool enough to handle. Peel each chile from the tip to the stem and discard the skins. If you are drying the chiles, leave them whole at this point and continue with the drying process. Otherwise, pull off the stems, remove the seeds and veins, and rinse in water to remove stray seeds.

The Open-Flame Method

Roast the whole fresh chiles over a barbecue grill or a gas stove with the flame set at medium-high. Turn the chiles with tongs every couple of minutes until all parts are thoroughly charred.

Remove the chiles from the flame and soak them in ice water. Under cold running water, rub the charred skins off and discard.

This method is a better one to use than the oven method when you are making stuffed chiles because the meat remains firm inside. If using a chile for stuffing or for cooking whole, leave on the stem and make only one slit to remove the veins and seeds, stuff the chile, and reseal it.

The Frying Method

Put 1 inch vegetable oil in a saucepan with sides high enough to protect you from spatters. Heat until hot but not quite smoking, then gently drop in enough chiles to cover the bottom of the pan. Turn with tongs as they begin to blister. The skins will loosen

as the chiles turn golden brown. Remove from oil and drain on paper towels. When the chiles are cool enough to handle, peel the skins from the stem to the tip and discard. Slice the chiles lengthwise, remove the seeds, devein, remove stems, and rinse.

NOTE: Whichever method you use, the chiles, once prepared, can be stored in plastic bags in the refrigerator for 3 days, or frozen and kept for up to 6 months.

Green chiles can also be dried for future use. Roast and peel the green chiles using the Oven Method (page 62). Hang the chiles on a long string or lay them flat on a screen and place outdoors for about 4 days (the weather must be warm and dry). Turn the chiles each day to make sure each side dries equally. Once the chiles are fully dried, they can be bagged and stored in a cool, dry place.

To reconstitute the dried chiles, soak them in warm water for ½ hour, then remove the stems and seeds The chiles will expand to their original size and can be used as you would use fresh chiles.

TESUQUE PUMPKIN COOKIES *(above) are a popular feast days offering.* **PUMPKIN-PIÑON BREAD** *(right) is delicious alone as a snack, or can be dressed up with pumpkin sauce and ice cream for a luscious dessert.*

Tesuque Pumpkin Cookies

Most of the pueblos in New Mexico are relatively close to one another. As I traveled throughout these pueblos I began to notice how similar some of the recipes were that were being shared with me. I then learned that many of the women bring prepared foods over to other pueblos as an act of graciousness during Feast Days or other celebrations. As a result, each pueblo has developed its own version of certain recipes.

I learned this particular recipe from the women of the Tesuque Pueblo just north of Santa Fe. The recipe yields seven dozen cookies and, if you choose, you can cut the recipe in half. But I advise you to bake the full amount. The cookies are delicious and not too sweet and will disappear faster than you could imagine!

2 cups sugar

2 cups vegetable shortening

2 cups Cooked Pumpkin (page 55)

2 eggs, beaten

2 teaspoons vanilla extract

4 cups all-purpose flour

2 teaspoons baking soda

1 teaspoon salt

1 teaspoon grated nutmeg

½ teaspoon ground allspice

2 cups raisins

1 cup chopped walnuts

Preheat the oven to 350° F. Grease a large cookie sheet.

In a large bowl, cream together the sugar and shortening. Add the pumpkin, eggs, and vanilla and beat until smooth.

In a separate bowl, combine the flour, baking soda, salt, nutmeg, and allspice.

Slowly add the dry ingredients to the pumpkin mixture, small amounts at a time, until completely mixed together. Stir in the raisins and walnuts.

Drop tablespoonfuls of the dough roughly 2 inches apart on the cookie sheet. Bake 12 to 15 minutes, until golden brown.

Makes approximately 7 dozen cookies

Pumpkin-Piñon Bread with Pumpkin Sauce and Ice Cream

This is a moist, dense bread that can be eaten alone like a tea bread, for a snack, or for breakfast. With the addition of the Pumpkin Sauce and Ice Cream, the bread can also be enjoyed as a wonderfully rich dessert.

PUMPKIN SAUCE AND ICE CREAM

20 egg yolks

2 cups sugar

2 quarts milk

½ vanilla bean, split down the middle

2 cups Cooked Pumpkin (page 55)

⅛ teaspoon ground cloves

⅛ teaspoon grated nutmeg

¼ teaspoon ground cinnamon

PUMPKIN-PIÑON BREAD

2 cups all-purpose flour

1 teaspoon baking soda

½ teaspoon salt

1½ cups sugar

2 teaspoons ground cinnamon

3 eggs, beaten

¾ cup milk

½ cup sunflower oil

1 teaspoon vanilla extract

2 cups Cooked Pumpkin (page 55)

1½ cups roasted piñons (see Note)

To make the pumpkin sauce and ice cream, beat the egg yolks and sugar together in a large bowl. Set aside.

Heat the milk and vanilla bean in a saucepan over high heat. Stir constantly until it almost reaches boiling point. Remove from the heat and slowly whisk the hot milk into the egg and sugar mixture. Return the mixture to the saucepan over medium-low heat and stir constantly about 10 minutes to thicken mixture. Do not allow mixture to boil or it will curdle.

Once the mixture is thick enough to coat the back of a spoon, remove it from the heat and add the pureed pumpkin. Stir until completely mixed.

Put 2 cups of the mixture in a bowl and add to it the ground cloves, nutmeg, and cinnamon. Mix together well and set over ice, stirring occasionally, until cool, then refrigerate. This pumpkin sauce will last up to 5 days refrigerated in a covered container.

Pour the remainder of the egg-pumpkin mixture into another bowl.

Set over ice, stirring occasionally, until it has cooled completely, then place in an ice cream machine and freeze according to the manufacturer's instructions. The ice cream will last several weeks in a covered container in the freezer.

To make the pumpkin bread, preheat the oven to 350° F. Sift together the flour, baking soda, salt, sugar, and cinnamon.

In a separate bowl, combine the eggs, milk, oil, and vanilla and mix well. Stir in the pumpkin puree and the dry ingredients, mix well, and fold in the piñons.

Pour the batter into 2 greased 5 x 9-inch loaf pans and bake 45 minutes, until the bread springs back when touched.

Serve with the Pumpkin Sauce and Ice Cream as dessert.

Makes 2 cups sauce; ½ gallon ice cream; and 2 5 x 9-inch loaves of bread; serves 12 as a dessert

NOTE: To roast piñons, also known as pine nuts, place them in a frying pan over medium heat and stir constantly so that they brown evenly, 3 to 5 minutes. No butter or oil is needed because the nuts contain natural oils.

WILD GREENS, FRUITS, CACTI, AND HERBS

The deserts and high mesas of Arizona and New Mexico are generously scattered with edible vegetation. Southwestern Native Americans, the ancient harvesters and gatherers, long ago discovered this abundance of edibles and have been using it ever since for medicinal and cooking purposes.

The aridity of the desert can cause a scarcity of many foods, but the wild plants that nature has given to this region are hardy enough to survive the long droughts and cold winters. Each spring the cacti bud, the fruits ripen, and the herbs and greens sprout anew. These signs of spring coincide with warmer days, increased sunshine, and a new beginning to the harvesting year.

Many greens grow wild in all parts of the Southwest, along highways and in pastures, amid desert rocks and beside planted gardens. Greens that in other parts of the country are available only in specialty markets — such as mâche (also known as lamb's quarters or *quelites*), or purslane (known to the Hopi as *peehala* and called *verdolagas* throughout New Mexico) — often can be found growing in southwestern backyards. Tumbleweed grows all over the parched, dry land; if picked in the spring and summer, when the plant is still young and green, the sprouts can be enjoyed as a vegetable in many dishes. Also commonly found growing wild in open fields and meadows are tart dandelion greens, spinach, and mustard greens. Native Americans traditionally did not use these greens in salads, but today, with increased nutritional awareness, they are being included in the diet as a complement to many dishes.

The different types of cacti produce wonderful edible fruits and blossoms. The yucca, found on mesas and foothills, blooms from May through October; its fruit, referred to as banana yucca, can be eaten fresh from the plant or cooked and eaten as a vegetable. The *cholla* cactus, found in the hotter regions of the desert, produces yellow and light-green buds that are still gathered with tongs by the Pima and Papago Indians of southern Arizona, as they were centuries ago. The fruit then is cooked and eaten as a vegetable. The prickly pear, the most popular edible cactus, produces reddish-magenta fruits in late summer to early fall. The tangy pulp is used for juices, jellies, preserves, and fruit ices. The pads of the cactus, known as *nopales*, are picked when young and green. Scraped clean of their spines, they can be eaten in a variety of dishes.

Fruits and berries are also seasonally harvested in the Southwest. Landscapes are adorned with juniper trees with ripening berries in the fall of every second year. The squawberry, a small reddish-colored tart berry, is used for a lemonadelike drink and in sauces that are usually served with game meats. Desert peaches, apricots, and apples are grown on the reservations by dry farming, and the resulting fruit is smaller but much sweeter than commercially grown fruit. During July and August the fruits ripen and are dried, eaten fresh, or made into jellies and syrups.

As I traveled around this arid region of America's Southwest, I was amazed at the abundant wild harvest I saw. Nature offers so much, and in such quantity. If you simply open your eyes, you can find it everywhere.

DANDELION GREEN SALAD *(left) and* **TUMBLEWEED, PINTO BEAN, AND WILD RICE SALAD** *(above) use harvest treasures.*

A goat cheese dressing is a contemporary addition to **YUCCA BLOSSOM SALAD** *(below).*

Dandelion Salad with Mustard Greens Vinaigrette

This combination of fresh greens, spicy chiles, and tender sweet baby corn is unusual and delicious.

DANDELION SALAD

2 red serrano or anaheim chiles

⅓ pound sunflower sprouts

20 ears baby corn (if not available fresh, use canned)

12 radishes

2 pounds dandelion greens, washed and stemmed

MUSTARD GREENS VINAIGRETTE

1 bunch mustard greens, washed and stemmed

1 cup sunflower oil

2 tablespoons herb-flavored vinegar

½ teaspoon salt

¼ teaspoon black pepper

Slice the chiles diagonally, remove seeds and veins, and stick small bunches of sprouts through the pieces.

Remove the husks and silk from the corn. Bring a small pot of water to a boil and cook the corn in it 1 minute. Drain, rinse in cold water, and cool. (If using canned corn, simply drain and rinse.) Wash and slice radishes.

To make vinaigrette, place mustard greens in a blender and add the remaining ingredients. Blend until smooth. Toss with salad greens and serve.

Serves 6

Tumbleweed, Pinto Bean, and Wild Rice Salad

Tumbleweed spreads quickly by tumbling across the sandy soil, scattering seeds that catch and sprout in depressions in the soil. The new young shoots must be picked when they are two to three inches tall, before they become dry and brittle and develop thornlike prickers.

To harvest them yourself, pick the sprouts from the base of the stem. Wash thoroughly until all the sand and dirt are removed. Drain and pat dry.

¾ cup dried pinto beans

1½ cups tumbleweed greens or curly endive, or fennel tops

1½ cups cooked wild rice

¾ cup sunflower oil

3 tablespoons herb-flavored red wine vinegar

2 tablespoons chopped fresh chives

2 small garlic cloves, peeled

¼ teaspoon black pepper

⅛ teaspoon salt

Chive blossoms, for garnish

Soak the beans overnight in water to cover. In the morning, drain the beans, rinse them under cold running water, and place them in a saucepan with fresh water to cover. Bring to a boil over high heat, then reduce the heat and simmer several hours until the beans are soft and the skins begin to split. Add water when necessary to keep the beans from drying, and stir

occasionally to prevent them from burning and sticking. Remove from the heat, drain, and allow to cool.

In a bowl, toss together the greens, beans, and rice. Cover and chill in the refrigerator at least 30 minutes.

In a blender, combine the oil, vinegar, chives, garlic, pepper, and salt. Blend at high speed until the chives and garlic are finely pureed.

Pour the dressing over the salad, toss, and garnish with chive blossoms.

Serves 6

Yucca Blossom Salad with Goat Cheese Dressing

At the end of the growing season, when the corn has matured, some of the ears that have been left on the plant develop a type of edible fungus the Indians call *cuitlacoche*. Inside each corn kernel is a moist, black paste that resembles caviar. It can be dried or canned and used throughout the year. Although it is not currently enjoyed by much of the younger generation of Native peoples, the elders consider *cuitlacoche* to be a delicacy.

YUCCA BLOSSOM SALAD
1 tablespoon olive oil
18 *cuitlacoche* (corn caviar) kernels, or other edible mushroom
30 yucca blossoms
6 cups mâche, stemmed; or Boston lettuce

GOAT CHEESE DRESSING
2 ounces (approximately ¼ cup) soft white goat cheese
¼ cup olive oil
½ teaspoon white pepper
¼ teaspoon salt
2 tablespoons herb-flavored vinegar

1 teaspoon chopped fresh thyme leaves

In a sauté pan, heat the oil over medium-low heat and sauté the *cuitlacoche* 1 to 2 minutes, stirring constantly, until tender. Set aside.

Fill a saucepan with water and bring to a boil. Blanch the yucca blossoms 20 to 30 seconds. Remove and immediately rinse the blossoms in ice water. Drain the flowers and remove the hearts. Set aside.

For the dressing, blend together all the ingredients, except the vinegar. Then, slowly mix in the vinegar drop by drop to avoid curdling, until all the vinegar has been incorporated.

Toss the salad together with the dressing and sprinkle the fresh thyme on top.

Serves 6

Summer Melon Fruit Salad with Prickly Pear Syrup

Several varieties of melons grown in the Southwest are enjoyed by Native Americans in late summer during cultural ceremonies and festivals. This recipe is cool and refreshing and a particular favorite of mine.

1 muskmelon or cantaloupe
10 fresh Indian peaches, or 5 commercially
    grown peaches
1 large prickly pear cactus pad (*nopale*)
¼ yellow watermelon (if not available, use pink
    watermelon)
Wild mint leaves, for garnish
¾ cup Prickly Pear Syrup (page 42)

Cut the muskmelon or cantaloupe in half and scoop out the seeds. Scoop the melon into 1-inch balls and place in a bowl. Cut the peaches in half, or with larger peaches, cut into slices. Add to the melon balls. Trim the cactus pad (see page 79), cut into strips, and blanch in boiling salted water 30 seconds to 1 minute. Rinse the pads under cool water to remove their gum; drain well. Toss together with the fruits.

Slice the watermelon in ½-inch slices and from each slice cut 1½-inch triangles, removing the seeds as you cut. (I have found that when you slice watermelon into pieces this size it is easier to make sure there are no seeds left.) Toss the watermelon with the other fruit.

Garnish with wild mint and serve with Prickly Pear Syrup.

Serves 12 as a salad or dessert

Sweet Watermelon Ice

This recipe makes a refreshing ice that is perfect for hot weather.

3 cups fresh Watermelon Juice (page 78)
3 tablespoons sugar
2 tablespoons freshly squeezed lemon juice

Pour the watermelon juice into a shallow glass baking dish. Add the sugar and lemon juice and stir well. Place the dish in the freezer and chill.

Remove the pan every ½ hour and stir. The juice will form light, grainy ice crystals as it freezes. Repeat this process until the juice is fully frozen, about 4 hours, depending on the temperature of your freezer. You can also use an ice cream maker, following the manufacturer's directions.

Serve immediately, or store in the freezer in a covered container up to several weeks.

Makes about 3 cups

SUMMER MELON FRUIT SALAD *should be served only when the fruits are at their peak.*

Watermelon Juice

Tribes all over the Southwest grow several different kinds of watermelons, the most popular of which are the watermelons with pink flesh and black seeds and the ones with yellow flesh and light pink seeds. Both are sweet and juicy and make a refreshing drink for warm weather.

It is believed that the Spanish introduced the watermelon to the Americas when they first arrived from Europe. Watermelons immediately became popular with the Native Americans because they are easy to grow, can be enjoyed fresh in the summer during harvest, and will last for months if stored whole in a cool, dry place — sometimes as late as March of the following year. They were, and still are, given as gifts at ceremonies, especially among the pueblo people.

1 10-pound watermelon, chilled

Slice the watermelon lengthwise into slices 1 to 2 inches thick. Carefully cut away the rind and discard. Place as much flesh as will fit into a food processor and process until smooth, about 15 seconds. Press through a fine sieve and discard seeds and pulp. Pour the juice into a pitcher. Repeat this process until all the watermelon has been blended and sieved. Chill and serve cold.

Makes about 10 cups

Navajo Peach Pudding

Traditionally, only Indian peaches and water are used. Although the simpler recipe is delicious, I have added honey, cream, and gelatin to create a richer taste and firmer consistency.

½ cup honey
1 pound fresh peaches, pitted and peeled
1 cup water
1 package unflavored gelatin
1 cup whipping cream

In a food processor, puree the honey and peaches together. Set aside.

In a small saucepan, mix together the water and gelatin and let stand 1 minute. Over medium-low heat, stir mixture until the gelatin has completely dissolved, about 5 minutes. Remove from heat, slowly add the gelatin mixture to the peach honey, and blend thoroughly. Allow to cool to room temperature, about 5 minutes.

While the peach mixture is cooling, beat the cream until firm peaks form, about 2 minutes.

Fold the whipped cream into the peach pudding mixture in a circular motion, leaving swirls of white cream in the peach pudding. Do not mix together completely.

Place the pudding in the refrigerator and chill until firm. Scoop out servings with a large spoon.

Serves 6

COOKING WITH THE PRICKLY PEAR CACTUS

The prickly pear cactus plant grows wild throughout the southern region of Arizona, where the air is warm and dry. It produces large, green, succulent pads that bear plump, juicy fruits in the late summer months.

Nopales

Prickly pear pads (*nopales*) have been eaten by the Native Americans for centuries. The pads are picked from the cactus but must be handled with care; the hairlike spines that project from the pads can easily get caught in your skin.

Cactus pads are found in most Mexican markets. It is better to choose the smaller and thicker deep-green pads because they are the most tender. Usually, fresh cactus pads are sold whole. For convenience, however, they may also be purchased in jars already diced and even precooked in their natural juices.

To clean the whole pads, hold them with a kitchen towel and remove the spines and rounded outside edge of the pads with a small paring knife or a vegetable peeler and discard.

Prickly Pear Fruits

Traditionally, prickly pear fruits are harvested in late summer. A brush made from wild grass is used to remove their fine, hairlike prickers and soft spines. To remove the prickers in a more conventional way, hold the fruit with metal tongs under cold running water and scrub the prickers off with a vegetable scrubbing brush.

When selecting fruits from the marketplace, be careful to choose those that are soft but not overripe. They may range in color from greenish-yellow to bright red, the latter being the ripest and best to eat. If the spines have not been removed, be careful when handling the fruits; the spines are small and difficult to remove from your hands. If only green fruits are available, store them at room temperature until they ripen to red.

To extract the juice from the fruits, wash them thoroughly under cold running water, cut off the ends, and cut in half lengthwise. Place them in a food processor and puree to a fine pulp. Press the pulp through a fine sieve, using a wooden spoon or spatula to remove the seeds, which should be discarded. Use the juice according to recipe instructions. Twelve prickly pears make approximately 1 cup of juice.

NOTE: The prickly pear fruit, because of its deep, rich color, is traditionally used by many tribes as a dye for thread used in their weavings. The juice from the fruit has a very powerful color and can stain clothing, utensils, and surfaces. You may want to wear an apron while preparing prickly pear fruits and use utensils that you don't mind getting stained.

CACTUS PAD SALAD WITH FIERY JALAPEÑO DRESSING *(left) is served on a coiled Apache basket-tray.* **AZAFRÁN SOUP** *contains fresh summer vegetables in a flavorful broth.*

Cactus Pad Salad with Fiery Jalapeño Dressing

On a warm summer day nothing is more appetizing than a light, refreshing salad. In this one, the pleasing sweetness of oranges balances the piquancy of the red peppers and the fiery flavor of the jalapeño dressing. The pumpkin seeds add a nice crunch.

CACTUS PAD SALAD

3 oranges
6 large cactus pads (*nopales*), trimmed (see page 79) and cut into 3-inch strips
3 red bell peppers
¼ cup pumpkin seeds, lightly toasted

FIERY JALAPEÑO DRESSING

6 tablespoons sunflower oil
3 tablespoons tarragon vinegar or other herb-flavored vinegar
½ teaspoon salt
¼ teaspoon black pepper
½ teaspoon red chile powder
2 green jalapeño peppers, seeded and finely chopped

Peel the oranges and cut into segments, removing the white pith.

Blanch the cactus pads in boiling salted water until they turn bright green, 30 seconds to 1 minute. Rinse thoroughly until the gum washes off the pads; drain well.

Roast, peel, and seed the bell peppers using one of the methods on pages 62–63. Cut into 3-inch strips.

In a bowl toss together the oranges, cactus pad strips, red pepper strips, and pumpkin seeds.

For the dressing, whisk together all the ingredients. Pour the dressing over the salad, toss, and serve.

Serves 6

Azafrán Soup with Spinach Greens and Yellow Cornmeal Dumplings

The subtle aromatic flavor of *azafrán* in this nutritious soup tastes wonderful with fresh, sweet vegetables. As well as adding it to certain recipes for flavor and color, the Native Americans historically used *azafrán* for medicinal purposes. Serve this as a main course or in smaller portions as an appetizer.

YELLOW CORNMEAL DUMPLINGS

1 cup ground yellow cornmeal
¾ cup all-purpose flour
2 teaspoons baking powder
1 teaspoon salt
1 teaspoon white pepper
2½ tablespoons sugar
1 teaspoon unsalted butter, softened
¾ cup milk
2 cups Chicken Stock (page 39)

AZAFRÁN SOUP

6 cups water
2 tablespoons *azafrán* (Native American saffron; see Note)
1 teaspoon salt

½ teaspoon white pepper

3 cups Chicken Stock (page 39)

2 yellow summer squash, diced

3 cups corn kernels

1 bunch spinach greens, washed and
stemmed

To make the dumplings, combine the cornmeal, flour, baking powder, salt, pepper, and sugar together in a bowl. Add the butter and milk and mix well to make a batter that is moist but not sticky. If the dough is too moist, knead in a little more flour. Divide the dough into 1-inch balls, flatten, and shape into small triangles.

Pour the chicken stock into a pot and bring to a boil over medium heat. Reduce the heat to a simmer and drop in the dumplings. Cook 3 to 4 minutes, until tender and cooked all the way through. Remove the dumplings from the stock and set aside.

For the soup, heat 2 cups of the water and the *azafrán* in a large saucepan over medium-high heat until the liquid has reduced by half, about 7 minutes. Pour through a fine sieve, discard the *azafrán*, and return the liquid to the saucepan. Add salt, pepper, stock, and the remaining 4 cups of the water and bring to a boil over medium-high heat. Add squash, reduce the heat, and simmer 5 minutes. Add corn kernels and simmer another 5 minutes. Add dumplings and spinach, cook 2 minutes, and serve immediately.

Serves 6

NOTE: *Azafrán*, also called Native American saffron by the American Indians, is an herb that is actually fine threads from the stigma of the safflower plant. Despite the name, *azafrán* is not the same as saffron, which is an expensive spice derived from the crocus plant in the iris family. (Saffron can be substituted for *azafrán*, though: use one pinch of saffron for two tablespoons of *azafrán*).

Azafrán is commonly sold in Latin American markets and specialty herb stores. It can also be ordered by mail (see Source Guide, page 153). It is best stored in a cool dark place and will last several months in a sealed plastic or glass container.

Brilliant red **PRICKLY PEAR ICE** *(left) and subtle yellow* **HOHOISE ICE** *(above) are refreshing endings to a rich meal.*

Prickly Pear Ice

This ice was traditionally served during the winter months using reconstituted prickly pears before refrigeration became available. The dessert was left outside overnight to freeze and enjoyed in the morning. Now, with refrigeration, the ice can be served year round and is particularly refreshing in the hot summer months.

1 cup water
1½ teaspoons freshly squeezed lemon juice
½ cup sugar
2¾ cups prickly pear juice (page 79)
2 cactus pads (*nopales*), scraped and trimmed (page 79) and cut into Indian motif shapes, for garnish

In a stainless steel or glass saucepan, bring the water and lemon juice to a boil over medium-high heat. Reduce the heat to low, add the sugar, and stir constantly until dissolved. Remove from the heat and stir in the prickly pear juice. Let cool.

Pour the liquid into a glass or stainless steel baking pan (do not use aluminum because the acid in the prickly pear juice will react with it) and place it in the freezer. Stir the liquid every 20 minutes until it has frozen into grainy, magenta-colored ice crystals. The process should take about 1½ hours, depending on the temperature of your freezer.

Serve with cactus pad garnish.

Serves 6

Hohoise Ice
(INDIAN TEA ICE)

During the spring and summer months on the high mesas of northern Arizona, a wild yellow flowering herb, called *hohoise* (Indian tea) by the Hopis, grows in abundance. It is quite common to see a solitary car stopped along a roadside and women picking *hohoise* in large bundles. While the herbs are still moist and pliable they are divided into small bundles, tied, and hung to dry for use throughout the year. *Hohoise* can be made into a tea, which has many excellent medicinal uses. For this recipe, I have added some spices to the tea and created an ice that is delicious enough for the children to enjoy.

1½ bundles *hohoise* leaves (see Note)
3 cups boiling water
¼ teaspoon ground cinnamon
1 cup sugar
½ teaspoon anise seed
2 cups water
6 star anise, for garnish
6 *hohoise* flowers, for garnish

To make the tea, add the bundles of *hohoise* leaves to the boiling water and continue to boil 2 minutes over high heat. Remove from the heat and let steep 10 minutes, covered. The liquid should turn a dark brown.

Add the cinnamon and sugar, mix well, and pour the liquid through a fine sieve to strain out the leaves and stems. Set aside.

Mix together the anise seed and 2 cups water and let sit for 5 minutes. Pour through a fine sieve to remove the seeds.

Mix the *hohoise* tea and the anise liquid together. Pour into a baking pan and place in the freezer. Every 20 minutes, remove the pan from the freezer and stir as the ice begins to crystalize. The liquid will freeze in about 2 hours. You can also use an ice cream maker, following the manufacturer's directions.

Garnish with the star anise and *hohoise* flowers.

Serves 6 as a dessert

NOTE: *Hohoise* can be obtained by mail order; see Source Guide (page 153). Otherwise, any other herb tea, or even plain tea, can be substituted.

Fresh Herb Jelly

There are many wild herbs and greens indigenous to the Southwest. Unfortunately, they may be difficult to obtain in other parts of the country, if available at all. This recipe has been adapted to include herbs available in commercial markets. You can also experiment with other fresh herbs according to your taste.

2 cups water
¾ cup freshly squeezed lemon juice
1 package (1¾ ounces) powdered pectin

4 cups sugar
¼ cup finely chopped fresh chives
¼ cup finely chopped fresh thyme leaves
¼ cup finely chopped fresh oregano leaves
¼ cup finely chopped fresh basil leaves
¼ cup finely chopped fresh tarragon leaves

In a large saucepan, stir together the water, lemon juice, and powdered pectin. Scrape the sides of the pan to make sure all the pectin has dissolved.

Place the saucepan over high heat and bring to a boil. Stir constantly to prevent scorching. Add the sugar and herbs while stirring. Bring the mixture to a full, rolling boil 4 minutes, then remove from the heat. Skim the foam off the top of the mixture and pour into clean, sterilized jars. Seal with paraffin, if desired, and allow to set overnight.

Makes 4 8-ounce jars of jelly

NOTE: If the herb jelly does not set overnight, remove the paraffin and reheat the mixture over high heat. Bring to a hard rolling boil 2 minutes, repour into the jars, and reseal. Because you are working with herbs and not fruit, sometimes the pectin doesn't react the first time and needs to be reboiled.

BEANS, NUTS AND SEEDS

Because beans, nuts, and seeds were relatively easy to grow, gather, and collect, they became increasingly important to the survival of the Native American people and their culture in an often harsh land. They were (and are) a major part of the daily diet, providing high quantities of proteins, carbohydrates, minerals, and vitamins. New strains of beans were developed and cultivated. Special pottery urns and jars were, and still are, used to store the harvest through the winter and unproductive seasons. Beans and seeds were also traded and even offered as gifts.

Some of these foods are native to the land and grow in wild abundance throughout the Southwest. Wild sunflowers with vivid yellow petals, for instance, produce seeds that are gathered and eaten. Traditionally, these seeds were carefully ground and then tossed into the air using sifter baskets so that the hulls would blow away in the wind. The leftover kernels were then ground into a meal or used whole.

The rolling hills of the northern territories of the Southwest are scattered with piñon trees that shed a nut-bearing cone. The piñon trees are somewhat unpredictable, however, and only bear their luscious nuts one season every four to seven years. But because the trees mature and bear fruit at different times in different areas of the hillsides, there are nuts to harvest every year.

The acorn is another rich-tasting nut found in the southern regions of Arizona. The Native American women collect these nuts in cloth flour sacks the same way they do piñons. I have seen Indian women seek shade underneath the tall oaks and gather nuts for hours while their children played nearby. When they have collected sufficient nuts, they journey home carrying the large sacks. Many of the nuts are stored and saved for winter use.

Beans are cultivated in great abundance throughout the Southwest and are highly valued among many of the tribes. The Native Americans have spent many years cultivating beans to produce a vast variety in many different colors. Especially prized are white, blue, red, yellow, multicolored, and black beans, which symbolize the six cardinal points: East, West, South, North, Zenith, and Nadir respectively.

Favored in Native American cooking are black, pinto, and different kinds of red beans. Each tribe has cultivated its own special variety of bean that does well in the soil of its own territory. Today, as part of a project dedicated to saving the many indigenous beans of the Southwest, researchers have introduced the anasazi bean—which has been widely used among the Native Americans but is virtually unheard of by the rest of America—to the commercial market. The tepary bean, which grows wild in southern Arizona and was once very popular among the Pima and Papago tribes, has also been introduced. (For all the recipes in this book, I have specified dried beans. Salt- and preservative-free canned beans can be substituted—for each cup dried beans, use 2 cups canned. But dried beans are always preferable.)

All of these foods—beans, nuts, and seeds—will continue to be an important and thriving part of the Native American diet. They are indeed sustenance in a pod.

GARBANZO BEAN STEW *(above) is served in many of the pueblos on their feast days.*

Two hearty soups, **BLACK BEAN SOUP AND CHIVE BLOSSOMS** *(below) and* **ACORN-PIÑON SOUP WITH WILD FLOWERS** *(right), are set against a southwestern-style hutch and Pueblo pottery.*

Garbanzo Bean Stew

Margaret Archuleta of Picuris Pueblo taught me the recipe for this simple and satisfying stew made with garbanzo beans. I first tasted it while celebrating New Year's Day with her family.

2 pounds dried garbanzo beans

10 cups water

4 pounds stew beef or venison, cut into 1-inch cubes

1 small onion, chopped

1 teaspoon salt

½ teaspoon white pepper

Soak the garbanzo beans overnight in twice their volume of water. The beans will absorb much of the water and swell in size. The following day, drain and rinse the beans under cold running water. Place the beans in a large pot with the 10 cups of water. Bring to a boil over high heat, reduce the heat to low, and simmer, uncovered, 1½ hours, stirring occasionally to prevent burning. Add the meat, onions, salt, and pepper, stir well, and continue cooking another 2 hours, until the meat is tender and the beans are fully cooked.

Serve hot with one of the many Indian breads, for example, Indian Tortillas (pages 141–142), Adobe Bread (page 146), or *Piki* Bread (page 148).

Serves 6 to 8

Black Bean Soup and Chive Blossoms with Homemade Tortilla Chips

This hearty soup is a favorite among many Indian families and is almost a meal in itself.

BLACK BEAN SOUP

1 pound dried black beans

1 tablespoon unsalted butter

1 cup finely chopped wild onions (see Note, page 59)

3 garlic cloves, peeled and crushed

1 teaspoon salt

¼ teaspoon black pepper

10 cups water

HOMEMADE TORTILLA CHIPS

4 corn tortillas, 6 inches in diameter

1 cup sunflower oil

½ cup coarsely ground blue cornmeal

Purple chive blossoms, chopped chives, and sour cream, for garnish

Soak the beans overnight in water to cover. The next day, drain the beans. Melt the butter in a large saucepan over medium heat, add the wild onions, and sauté until translucent, about 3 minutes. Add the garlic, sauté 1 more minute, and add the drained beans, salt, pepper, and 4 cups of the water. Bring to a boil over high heat, then reduce the heat and simmer, covered, 30 minutes, stirring occasionally to avoid burning the beans.

Add 4 more cups water and cook, uncovered, another 30 minutes, again stirring occasionally.

Add the remaining 2 cups water and cook 20 minutes, until the beans are soft but still firm.

While the beans are cooking, prepare the tortilla chips. Stack the tortillas on a work surface. With a sharp knife, cut the round tortillas into 3 interlocking triangles.

Heat the oil over medium-high heat in a skillet until it is very hot but not smoking. Carefully place each tortilla triangle in the oil; be careful of splatters. Allow the tortillas to cook 30 seconds and, with a fork, turn the tortillas over, then repeat the process with the remaining tortillas.

Remove the chips from the oil and dip a corner of each chip into the blue cornmeal. Place on a paper towel to drain off excess oil.

Garnish the soup with the chips, purple chive blossoms, and chopped chives. Serve hot with the sour cream on the side.

Serves 6

Acorn-Piñon Soup with Wild Flowers

Traditionally, this recipe is prepared with the small, brown acorns of the Emery oaks that are indigenous to the Chiricahua Mountains in the southeastern part of Arizona. The Apache tribes originally lived in this region before they were relocated northeast to San Carlos.

1 tablespoon unsalted butter
1 cup piñons (pine nuts)
4 tablespoons shelled acorns, or unsalted pistachio nuts
6 tablespoons chopped wild onions (see Note, page 59) or leeks
9 cups Chicken Stock (page 39) or Rabbit Stock (page 130)
¼ teaspoon salt
½ teaspoon black pepper
1½ quarts half-and-half
Snipped wild onions, mint sprigs, and wild edible flowers, for garnish

Melt the butter in a large saucepan over medium heat and sauté the piñons, acorns, and onions 4 minutes, until the onions are translucent and the nuts golden brown.

Add the stock, salt, and pepper. Bring to a boil, then reduce the heat to medium and cook until the mixture is reduced by half, about 20 minutes. Add the half-and-half and reduce the mixture again by half, to 6 cups.

Remove from the heat and blend in a blender or food processor until the mixture is smooth. Push through a fine sieve; discard the contents of the sieve. Garnish with the mint, wild onions, and edible flowers and serve.

Serves 6

The **INDIAN BEAN TERRINE IN BROWN HERB SAUCE WITH BLUE CORNMEAL TORTILLA FEATHERS** *(left) reflects the hues and tones visible in the desert.*

ANASAZI AND PINTO BEANS WITH HOMINY AND GREEN CHILES *(above) is a southwestern staple.*

Indian Bean Terrine in Brown Herb Sauce with Blue Cornmeal Tortilla Feathers

This hearty terrine can be served either as an appetizer or as a main course accompanied by a salad. Because the terrine is a bit time consuming to prepare, I usually make it a day in advance and reheat it just before the meal is served. This enhances the flavor of the dish and allows the terrine to set fully.

INDIAN BEAN TERRINE

1 pound dried small white or pinto beans

1 tablespoon unsalted butter

½ cup yellow cornmeal

2 cups water

1 teaspoon salt

⅛ teaspoon white pepper

½ teaspoon red chile powder

1 teaspoon ground cumin

BROWN HERB SAUCE

3 cups Veal Stock (page 38)

4 tablespoons (½ stick) unsalted butter, softened

2 tablespoons chopped fresh tarragon

3 tablespoons chopped fresh chives

2 tablespoons chopped fresh dill

2 tablespoons chopped fresh basil

32 sprigs fresh chervil, for garnish

8 whole chives, for garnish

BLUE CORNMEAL TORTILLA FEATHERS

8 Blue Cornmeal Tortillas (page 141)

1 cup vegetable oil

Soak the beans overnight in enough water to cover. The following day, drain the beans, rinse under cold running water, and place in a pot with fresh water to cover. Bring to a boil over high heat, then reduce heat and simmer for several hours until the beans are soft. Remove from heat and drain. Mash the beans and mix with butter and cornmeal. Set aside.

Bring the 2 cups of water to a boil over high heat. Add the bean mixture, salt, pepper, chile powder, and cumin. Reduce the heat and simmer 20 minutes, stirring occasionally to prevent burning. Pour into a greased 5 x 9-inch loaf pan, cool to room temperature, and chill in the refrigerator overnight or until firm. Unmold from the loaf pan, cut into approximately ½-inch slices, and set on a cookie sheet. Reheat in a 350° F. oven for 10 minutes, until warm.

For the Brown Herb Sauce, bring the stock to a boil in a large saucepan over moderate heat. Add the butter and stir until completely melted. Add the tarragon, chives, dill, and basil, stir 1 minute, and remove from heat.

Cut the tortillas into feather shapes with scissors or a small paring knife. In a skillet over moderate to high heat, heat the oil until it almost reaches the smoking point. Using two forks, dip each tortilla feather into the hot oil, remove, and blot dry with a paper towel.

Spoon some Brown Herb Sauce

onto each plate and place 2 slices of the Indian Bean Terrine in the center. Garnish with a Blue Cornmeal Tortilla Feather, a whole chive, and sprigs of fresh chervil.

Serves 8

Anasazi and Pinto Beans with Hominy and Green Chiles

Most southwestern Indians grow beans. The Hopis grow a variety of beans in terraces along their high mesas, where the crop is irrigated by natural springs. After the harvest the beans are dried and stored. Some beans are used for ceremonial purposes — from weddings to Kachina dances — while others are used for their day-to-day meals.

For suburban and city dwellers I've found that pinto beans, white beans, or red beans work well, but I suggest you also experiment with some of the other varieties of beans — like anasazi beans — that are now available commercially. Or you may want to be adventuresome and grow your own variety.

To round out this meal, the beans can be served with Lamb-Stuffed Green Chiles (page 122), Pan-Fried Trout (page 134), or Venison Steaks (page 114) and one of the many Indian breads such as *Piki* Bread (page 148), Indian Frybread (page 150), or Adobe Bread (page 146).

1½ cups dried anasazi beans (see Note)
1½ cups dried pinto beans
10 cups water
1 teaspoon salt
3 cups dried Indian Hominy (page 21)
3 green anaheim chiles, for garnish

Soak the beans overnight in water to cover. In the morning rinse the beans with cold water and place in a large pot with fresh water to cover. Stir in the salt, cover, and simmer slowly 2 to 2½ hours, until the beans are tender. Add water when necessary and stir occasionally to prevent the beans from burning.

Add hominy and simmer, covered, 1 hour, stirring occasionally. The hominy and beans should be soft and moist but not too watery.

While the beans and hominy are cooking, roast, peel, seed, and dice the chiles (pages 62–63). Sprinkle on top of the cooked beans for garnish.

Serves 6 to 8

NOTE: *Anasazi*, Navajo for "the ancient ones," is the name given to the Native Americans who created the cliff dwellings in the Southwest. The sweet-tasting anasazi bean, one of the first foods cultivated by Native Americans, is high in protein and other nutrients. It also has a beautiful color.

Native American motifs are used to enhance the presentation of the **APACHE ACORN RAVIOLI IN CLEAR BROTH** *(left). The flavors of the spicy* **PINTO BEAN RAVIOLI WITH CORN AND CHILE CREAM SAUCE** *(above) give away its origin.*

Spicy Pinto Bean Ravioli with Corn and Chile Cream Sauce

This recipe combines many simple ingredients commonly used in Native American cooking. Although ravioli are quite familiar to most people, these, made from blue cornmeal, have a heavier, more granular texture. They are filled with a zesty bean puree flavored with several herbs and red chile powder.

SPICY PINTO BEAN RAVIOLI

2 cups dried pinto beans

1 teaspoon dried oregano

1 teaspoon ground cumin

4 garlic cloves, unpeeled

1 small onion, chopped

¼ cup vegetable oil or lard

1 tablespoon red chile powder

1 teaspoon salt

1 recipe Blue Cornmeal Ravioli Dough (see Variation, page 106)

1 egg, beaten, for egg wash

CORN AND CHILE CREAM SAUCE

6 green anaheim chiles

4 cups corn kernels

3 serrano chiles, seeded and chopped

1 teaspoon salt

½ teaspoon white pepper

2 cups heavy cream

Red chiles, for garnish

Green chiles, for garnish

Soak the beans overnight in water to cover. In the morning rinse the beans with cold water and place them in a saucepan with enough fresh water to cover. Bring to a boil over high heat, then reduce heat and simmer several hours, until the beans become soft and the skins begin to split. Add water when necessary and stir occasionally to prevent the beans from burning. Remove from the heat.

To prepare the bean puree, toast the oregano and cumin in a dry sauté pan over medium heat until lightly browned. Remove from the pan and set aside. Add the unpeeled garlic to the pan and roast over medium heat until it is soft and blackened in spots. Let cool, then peel and mash with a knife.

In a saucepan, sauté the onion in 1 tablespoon of the oil over moderate heat until it is lightly browned. Reduce the heat to low, add the garlic, and cook 1 minute. Add the oregano, cumin, chile powder, salt, beans, and just enough water to cover, 2 to 3 cups. Bring to a boil over high heat then reduce heat and simmer, uncovered, 30 minutes.

Puree the bean mixture in a food processor until smooth.

In a cast-iron skillet, heat the remaining oil over high heat to its smoking point. Add the bean puree and stir 1 minute. Reduce the heat to moderate and cook 5 minutes, while stirring, until the bean puree is a medium paste. It will thicken as it cools.

Next prepare the ravioli dough following the directions on page 106. Divide the dough in half and roll out each portion of the dough ⅛-inch thick into a rectangle 12 x 15 inches. With the back of a knife lightly mark 3-inch squares into the dough. With a basting brush, spread a thin layer of egg wash about 1-inch wide along the marked lines on the dough. Place 1 tablespoon bean filling in the center of each square with a spoon.

Roll out the remaining dough to the same size as the bottom layer and place on top. With your fingers press down around each mound of filling to release the air and seal each piece of ravioli. Cut between the mounds with a pasta crimper and sealer, making sure the top and bottom layer of the pasta dough are sealed securely. Set the ravioli aside while you make the sauce.

To make the cream sauce, roast the anaheim chiles (pages 62–63), then peel, seed, devein, and dice them. Combine 3 cups of the corn, ⅔ of the diced anaheim chiles, the serrano chiles, salt, and pepper in a food processor and process about 2 minutes, until smooth. Scrape the sides and process another 30 seconds. Push through a fine sieve and discard the skins.

Put the mixture in a saucepan and heat over moderate heat 3 minutes, slowly adding the cream while stirring. Add the remaining corn kernels and diced anaheim chiles. Reduce the heat to low and simmer 5 minutes until the corn is tender. Set aside to keep warm.

Fill a large pot with water and bring to a boil. Place the ravioli in the water and cook 3 to 5 minutes, until tender.

Drain the ravioli and serve immediately with the cream sauce. Allow 2 to 3 ravioli per person. Garnish with red and green chiles.

Serves 6 as a first course

Apache Acorn Ravioli in Clear Broth

During my travels throughout the southern Apache lands of Arizona, I was introduced to the acorns of the Emery oak (*quercus emoryi*) and taught how to gather and harvest them. Much lower in tannic acid than the acorns of other oaks, this is a rich-tasting nut that is commonly eaten as a snack. It can be easily cracked with your teeth, like a sunflower seed, if you bite down on the outside shell. When working with acorns in your kitchen, place them on a flat wood surface and firmly press the flat side of a large knife (as you would garlic) on top of the nuts to break them open. Then simply peel the shells away and use according to cooking instructions.

The acorn is used in a variety of recipes, but this one is a personal favorite — a modern adaptation based on traditional methods.

APACHE ACORN RAVIOLI

2 green anaheim chiles

1 tablespoon unsalted butter

1 tablespoon shelled and finely chopped acorns
   or unsalted pistachio nuts

3 to 4 ounces (⅓ cup) soft white goat cheese

1 recipe Basic Egg Ravioli Dough (page 106)

2 teaspoons kosher salt

1 quart water

CLEAR BROTH

6 cups Chicken Stock (page 39) or Rabbit Stock
   (page 130)

1 scallion, green part only, diagonally sliced

½ teaspoon *azafrán* (see Note, page 83)

Roast the chiles (see pages 62–63), then peel, seed, devein, and coarsely chop them.

Melt the butter in a saucepan over medium-low heat and add the acorns. Sauté 3 minutes, stirring constantly. Add the green chiles and sauté another minute. Remove from the heat, mix together with the goat cheese, and set aside.

Prepare a stencil by cutting a design out of a piece of cardboard. For the ravioli in the photograph we cut a stencil 5 inches in length, 3 inches in height, with 1-inch steps.

Roll out the ravioli dough as thinly as possible. Fold the dough in half, place the stencil over the dough and, with a sharp knife, cut around it. Repeat this process 11 times to make 24 identical pieces of dough.

Lay 12 cut-out pieces of dough on a board and place about 1 tablespoon of the acorn filling in the center of each. Moisten the outer edges of each piece of the dough. Place the other 12 pieces on top, and press the edges together with your fingers. If the edges are slightly uneven, trim them. Set aside.

Add the salt to the water in a wide, large saucepan and bring to a boil over high heat. Add the ravioli and cook 3 minutes, until tender and translucent around the edges. Drain and set aside.

Bring the stock to a boil in a large saucepan over medium-high heat. Add the scallions and *azafrán* and simmer, uncovered, over medium-low heat 5 minutes.

Remove from the heat and pour 1 cup of the broth into each bowl. Add some ravioli and serve.

Serves 6 as a first course

FEAST DAYS PIÑON TORTE *is decorated with stenciled Native American motifs.*

Basic Egg Ravioli Dough

It is customary for the Native American woman to knead and roll her own dough. Usually a group of women get together to prepare dough for some special gathering or feast. Although they usually make enough only for the day's event, a sufficient amount can be prepared and stored for several meals. If wrapped in wax paper, the dough will last several weeks in the refrigerator and several months in the freezer.

This basic dough makes excellent ravioli, which can be stuffed with a variety of different ingredients and used for appetizers, soups, and main courses.

Mixing and kneading the dough can be done with bare hands, just as the Native Americans do. Rolling out can also be done by hand, or you can use a pasta machine.

3 cups sifted all-purpose flour
4 eggs
1 teaspoon salt
1 teaspoon vegetable oil

Pour the flour into a mound on a flat working surface. Make a depression in the center with your hand that almost reaches through to the board. Crack the eggs directly into the well and, with a fork, whip in the salt and oil, mixing the flour in from around the edges.

Mix and knead the dough with your hands 8 to 10 minutes, until the dough has a smooth and elastic consistency. If the dough seems a bit dry, add a little water; add a little more flour if it seems too moist. Once you have obtained the desired consistency, cover the dough with plastic wrap and place it in the refrigerator 15 minutes.

Divide the dough into handfuls and roll out each section to a very thin, even, almost translucent thickness.

Use your imagination to cut the dough into any size or shape. Any filling can be used to make the ravioli.

Makes 12 large raviolis

VARIATION:

To make blue cornmeal ravioli, substitute a combination of 1 cup finely ground blue cornmeal and 1½ cups flour for the flour in this recipe. Increase the number of eggs to 5.

Feast Days Piñon Torte

The Feast Day is one of the biggest celebrations of the year among the Indian pueblos of New Mexico. To honor their patron saints, the people of each pueblo gather together. They attend mass in the morning and then, dressed in ceremonial costume, they spend the rest of the day performing ancient traditional dances in the plaza.

After mass, many of the women return home to prepare the day's feast

and set the special dishes up on tables with chairs crowded around them. On each table is a variety of salads, stews, meats, homemade breads, and, of course, desserts — both traditional as well as modern dishes.

During the afternoon, as the dances are going on in the plaza, relatives and visitors drop in and enjoy what food is offered, express their thanks, and leave to go back to the dances. People drop in throughout the day to taste the fine foods at many different houses. It is a festive day filled with warmth and friendliness.

This recipe is my adaptation of some of the tortes I sampled at different pueblos.

1 cup piñons (pine nuts)

2 tablespoons blue cornmeal

2 tablespoons unsalted butter

9 ounces semi-sweet chocolate

6 egg yolks

¾ cup granulated sugar

1 teaspoon vanilla extract

¼ cup confectioners' sugar and 2 tablespoons blue cornmeal, for decoration (optional)

Grease and flour a 9-inch round cake pan. Preheat the oven to 350° F.

In a food processor, grind the piñons to a moist nutmeal. Add the cornmeal and blend again about 30 seconds, just long enough to combine.

In a double boiler over medium-high heat, melt the butter and chocolate together, stirring occasionally so that they melt and blend evenly. Add to the piñon mixture in the food processor and blend about 1 minute, until smooth.

Beat the egg yolks, sugar, and vanilla together in a bowl, and add to the other ingredients in the food processor. Blend again until smooth.

Pour the batter into the prepared pan and bake 20 minutes, or until the cake is firm and springs back when the center is touched. Remove from the oven and place on a wire rack to cool before decorating.

When the torte has cooled, after 20 to 30 minutes, remove it from the pan, then be creative for the decorating process. To make the southwestern motif pictured, cut a stencil out of cardboard. First dust the cake with confectioners' sugar using a medium sieve, lightly tapping the sides and moving it in a circular motion around the surface of the torte. Then carefully hold the stencil as close to the torte's surface as possible without touching it and sprinkle the blue cornmeal through a sieve over the exposed areas. Carefully remove the stencil without disrupting the design. For a finishing touch, place a few piñons at the corner of each stenciled triangle.

Serves 6

GAME BIRDS,
MEATS,
AND FISH

Throughout history, Native Americans have been known for their ability to live solely off what the land provides. Cultivators and harvesters of many foods, they are also skilled hunters of game. They treat their land and the land's creatures with respect and gratitude, however. Before a hunter goes out in pursuit of game, he prays that an animal be provided for him so he can nourish himself and his family. The Native American believes that when a hunter partakes in the hunting of game meat, he is not only feeding his family but he is also sharing a oneness with the spirit of the animal.

Today hunting has more of a ceremonial and spiritual purpose. But still, when game is hunted and brought home, respect for the animal is important. Every part of the animal is utilized — the meat for nourishment and the hides, skins, and feathers for clothing worn for traditional dances and medicinal rituals. To ensure that the ancient hunting methods are preserved for the generations to come, children are taught to use the bow and arrow, still an integral part of the ceremonial dances.

Now, hunting has restrictions. Permits are required in most areas, and the hunting of some species is prohibited except in certain seasons. Throughout the Southwest, however, hunting is still widely practiced, using both traditional and modern techniques. And, the celebration after a successful hunt is still as joyous and festive as it has been for generations.

Each region of the Southwest has different varieties of game birds, meats, and fish. Game birds such as dove and quail are abundant in the desert and in the higher altitudes of the forest regions. They are commonly hunted and are frequently used in Native American recipes. Jackrabbits are commonly seen throughout the desert regions and are featured in many different dishes.

On Navajo land, sheep are still very common. Many families raise their own herds; they use the sheep and lamb meat for food and the wool for weaving. Many Navajos are master weavers; their blankets usually tell stories of a family's past or present life. Sheep were and still are a sign of wealth and stability in a Navajo family. They are even given as a dowry to a young girl's family from her prospective husband.

Larger game animals such as elk and deer are abundant in the higher mountainous regions of the Southwest. The meat is used in various recipes and made into jerky, the hides are used for clothing, and the antlers are made into buttons or jewelry.

Many pueblos are located along the Rio Grande, where the waters flow with an abundance of fresh fish. Therefore fish has become an important part of the Native American diet. It took great skill and patience to catch fish using the primitive methods first devised by the Native Americans many years ago; today, although the old ways are still taught, more modern methods are commonly used.

These often parched and desolate lands are surprisingly filled with life. The Native Americans respect the land and in return have been rewarded with everything that the land has to offer.

APACHE STEW *(left) was traditionally prepared over an open fire. Today it is common to see it prepared this way for camp groups gathered for such ceremonies as the Sunrise Dance.*

The flavor of **VENISON** *is enhanced by grilling the steaks over an open fire (above).*

Apache Stew

The Apache people lived in many regions throughout southeastern Arizona and New Mexico. The men hunted the animals that roamed the mountains, and the women gathered and harvested both wild foods and the foods that they cultivated on the land.

This recipe is based on a traditional stew that was taught to me by a San Carlos medicine man during one of my visits to his ranch. When I prepare the stew now, I can vividly remember the tapping of his traditional water drum and the songs he chanted in his native Apache tongue. Through his songs, he asked for all people to walk in harmony with Mother Earth and be guided by the spirit of the mountains and the spirit of his drum. I still remember the sincerity and yearning of his songs.

Depending on what type of produce was available, the ingredients added to the venison varied each time the stew was prepared. This recipe includes the basics of the stew, but you can substitute other vegetables.

2 red bell peppers
5 green anaheim chiles
¼ cup sunflower oil
1 pound venison, cut into 1½-inch cubes
1 onion, diced
3 garlic cloves, finely chopped
2 carrots, sliced
3 cups cooked Indian Hominy (page 21)
8 cups water
1½ teaspoon salt
1 teaspoon white pepper
1 cup tumbleweed greens (see page 74), thoroughly cleaned, or curly endive

Roast the peppers (pages 62–63), then peel, seed, and cut into long strips. Roast the chiles (pages 62–63), then peel, seed, devein, and dice.

Heat the oil in a large stew pot over medium-high heat. When the oil is almost smoking, add the venison and cook until the meat is lightly browned, 3 to 5 minutes. Add the onion and garlic and sauté 2 minutes more.

Stir in the carrots, peppers, and chiles and cook 1 minute more. Add the hominy, water, salt, and pepper and bring the mixture to a boil. Reduce the heat to low and let the stew simmer 1½ hours, stirring occasionally to avoid burning, until the meat is very tender. Just before serving, add the tumbleweed greens, stir 1 minute, and spoon into bowls.

Serves 8 to 10

Venison Steaks with Juniper Berry and Fiery Red Chile Sauce

In the high-altitude areas of the Southwest venison is a game meat widely eaten by Native Americans. Until recently, wild venison could only be obtained by cooks with a hunter in the family. Now it can be

obtained by mail order (see Source Guide, page 153).

This recipe is prepared over an open grill, which enhances the delicious gamy flavor of the venison.

JUNIPER BERRY AND FIERY RED CHILE SAUCE

2 tablespoons dried juniper berries (see Note 1)

3 cups dry red wine (see Note 2)

2 bay leaves

1½ teaspoons dried thyme

2 shallots, peeled and coarsely chopped

2 cups Veal Stock (page 38)

4 whole dried chiles de árbol

VENISON STEAKS

6 venison steaks, 8 to 10 ounces each

2 tablespoons olive oil

1 tablespoon salt

1 tablespoon black pepper

To make the sauce, wrap the juniper berries in a kitchen towel and crush them using a heavy skillet or mallet. Remove them from the towel and place them in a saucepan with the red wine, bay leaves, thyme, and shallots. Simmer over medium heat about 20 minutes, until the liquid has reduced to 1 cup.

Add the Veal Stock and simmer over medium heat another 15 minutes, until the sauce has reduced to 1½ cups.

While the stock is reducing, place the chiles in small bowl and remove their stems and seeds. With your fingers, tear the chiles into small pieces about the size of small beans. Set aside.

Remove the sauce from the heat and pass it through a fine sieve to remove the herb leaves and berry skins.

Heat coals in an open grill to a fiery hot temperature.

Brush each steak on both sides with the olive oil and season with salt and pepper.

Place the steaks on the grill and cook about 3 minutes, until they have charred marks. Rotate the steaks a half-turn and grill another 3 minutes, until the steaks have a cross-hatched charred pattern.

Flip the steaks over and grill about 5 minutes more, until done as desired.

Ladle the sauce onto each plate, top with steaks, patterned side up, and sprinkle with the dried red chile peppers.

Serves 6

NOTE 1: Juniper berries gathered on the reservation have a light and delicate flavor; commercially sold berries tend to be more aromatic and pungent. If you use store-bought berries, use half the amount of berries.

NOTE 2: On many reservations today alcohol is prohibited, and so it is not customary to use it in cooking. Wine reductions, however, add a marvelous flavor to sauces. If you wish to be traditional, you can substitute unsweetened grape juice for the wine. This will change the flavor of the sauce, but it will still taste good.

VENISON HASH WITH QUAIL EGGS AND BACON *(left) makes a hearty breakfast.*

A filling **WILD MINT AND LAMB SOUP** *(above) is served in a Tularosa plainware bowl from the Mogollon Culture of eastern Arizona (ca. 1100–1250).*

Venison Hash with Quail Eggs and Bacon

Many people believe that a nutritious, well-balanced breakfast is the most important meal of the day. Breakfast fuels the body and gives us the energy we need to take on the day's activities. Using ingredients commonly found in the Southwest, I have combined a traditional recipe for venison hash with an Indian version of the "all American" bacon-and-eggs breakfast.

VENISON HASH

3 tablespoons unsalted butter
1½ pounds venison, cubed
1 onion, chopped
3 stalks celery, chopped
3 large Russet potatoes, diced
1 tablespoon salt
1 tablespoon black pepper
1 cup water

QUAIL EGGS AND BACON

12 quail eggs
Vegetable oil
¾ pound bacon, thickly sliced

Melt the butter in a large skillet over medium-high heat and brown the venison about 2 minutes while stirring constantly. Add the onions, celery, and potatoes and stir another 2 minutes. Add the salt, pepper, and water and bring to a boil. Reduce the heat and simmer, covered, 1½ to 2 hours. Stir the hash occasionally to avoid burning and to keep it from sticking to the bottom of the pan.

Cook the bacon in a skillet over medium-low heat about 6 minutes, until golden brown and crisp. Remove from the pan and drain on paper towels.

Coat the bottom of a large pan with vegetable oil and carefully crack the eggs into the pan. Cook over moderate heat until the egg whites are solid and the yolks are cooked to the desired consistency.

Remove carefully with a spatula and serve hot with the hash and quail eggs.

Serves 6

Wild Mint and Lamb Soup

On a cold, wintry night a steaming bowl of hearty soup can warm the chill within. This one, with a touch of wild mint, is also very delicious.

Wild mint was customarily picked during the summer, when the herb is in season, and hung to dry in bundles in the sun. During the winter the stored dried mint adds a refreshing tang to many different dishes.

Traditionally, this recipe is made with mutton, but I have substituted lamb because of its superior tenderness, taste, and availability.

1 pound lamb stew meat, cut into 1-inch cubes
1 teaspoon salt

½ teaspoon black pepper

1 tablespoon olive oil

1 cup diced carrots

1 cup diced celery

2 tablespoons chopped mint leaves (fresh or dried)

4 cups water

4 cups Lamb Stock (page 119)

Wild mint leaves, for garnish

Season the lamb with salt and pepper.

In a skillet, heat the olive oil over medium-high heat and add the meat. Brown 3 minutes on each side until the lamb is medium-rare. Remove the meat from the pan and set aside.

Add the carrots and celery to the skillet and sauté over moderate heat 2 minutes, stirring constantly. Remove from the heat and add the chopped mint.

Pour the water into a large pot, add the vegetables from the pan, and bring to a boil over high heat. Reduce the heat and simmer 15 minutes. Add the stock and bring to a boil again over high heat. Reduce the heat and simmer 10 minutes. Add the meat and bring to a boil once again over high heat. Garnish with wild mint leaves and serve hot with one of the traditional Indian breads.

Serves 6

Lamb Stock

5 pounds lamb shank bones or lamb loin bones

1 tablespoon olive oil

5 ripe tomatoes, quartered

2 leeks, coarsely chopped

5 celery stalks, coarsely chopped

4 large carrots, coarsely chopped

6 quarts water

4 bay leaves

1 bunch fresh parsley

2 bunches fresh thyme

2 bunches fresh rosemary

Preheat the oven to 450° F. Put the bones in a large roasting pan and brown in the oven about 1 hour, turning them every 20 minutes. Remove from the oven and set aside.

In a large stock pot heat the olive oil, add tomatoes, leeks, celery, and carrots, and sauté over high heat 15 minutes, stirring constantly.

Add the bones, water, and herbs and bring to a boil over medium heat. Reduce the heat and simmer 4½ to 5 hours, skimming the surface every half hour.

Remove from the heat and pour the stock through a sieve lined with cheesecloth. Discard the contents of the sieve.

Refrigerate the stock 3 hours, then remove the solidified fat from the top. The stock will keep 5 days in a covered container in the refrigerator or for several months in the freezer.

Makes 4 quarts

LAMB STUFFED GREEN CHILES *(left) are another southwestern adaptation of a familiar recipe.* **STUFFED QUAIL** *(above) is accompanied by a tart squawberry sauce.*

Lamb-Stuffed Green Chiles with Fresh Tomato Puree

This recipe, an adaptation of stuffed green peppers, combines many regional ingredients that grow wild throughout the land.

LAMB-STUFFED GREEN CHILES

12 firm green anaheim chiles
1 tablespoon cooking oil
⅔ cup finely chopped wild onions (see Note, page 59) or yellow onions
1½ pounds ground lamb
1 cup Adobe Bread Crumbs (page 146)
2 ripe tomatoes, coarsely chopped
2 garlic cloves, finely chopped
1 teaspoon white pepper
½ teaspoon salt
½ teaspoon dried thyme
2 bay leaves
1 teaspoon dried tarragon

FRESH TOMATO PUREE

1¼ pounds ripe tomatoes, coarsely chopped
1 garlic clove, finely chopped

Roast, peel, and seed chiles, keeping them whole, according to the directions on pages 62–63. Set aside.

Heat the oil in a large skillet over medium heat and sauté the onions about 4 minutes, until translucent. Add the ground lamb and brown 15 minutes, stirring occasionally to prevent burning. Drain off the excess fat and add the bread crumbs, tomatoes, gar-lic, pepper, salt, and herbs. Reduce the heat and simmer another 30 minutes. Remove and discard the bay leaves. Remove the mixture from the heat and let cool.

Slice the chiles lengthwise, spread them open on a work surface and generously stuff each chile with the mixture. Set aside.

To make the sauce, combine the tomatoes and garlic in a saucepan and cook over medium-low heat 15 minutes, stirring occasionally, until the excess liquid evaporates. Remove from the heat and pour through a fine sieve. Heat again over medium heat until the sauce reduces and is thick, about 5 minutes. Set aside.

Preheat the oven to 350° F. Place the stuffed chiles in a baking dish and warm in the oven 5 to 10 minutes. Serve immediately with the tomato puree.

Serves 6

Stuffed Quail with Squawberry Sauce

In some parts of the Southwest, wild quail are still hunted with bow and arrow. Squawberries are the pungent, lemony berries, similar to juniper berries, of a Southwestern shrub; their flavor is infused into the sauce, but they are not eaten. You can substitute pink peppercorns.

STUFFED QUAIL

6 baby quail

1 cup crumbled White Sage Bread (page 147)

½ cup cooked corn kernels

½ cup shelled black walnuts, very finely chopped

1 tablespoon chopped fresh chives

1 tablespoon chopped fresh sage leaves

⅛ teaspoon salt

⅛ teaspoon black pepper

⅓ cup Veal Stock (page 38)

2 tablespoons unsalted butter, melted

SQUAWBERRY SAUCE

1 cup cold water

¼ cup squawberries or pink peppercorns
   (see Note)

1½ cups Veal Stock (page 38)

4 tablespoons (½ stick) unsalted butter

Whole sage leaves, for garnish

Prepare each quail by splitting it down the backbone, leaving the breast-bone intact, and cutting off the legs where they meet the body. You should have 3 separate pieces: the body and the pair of legs. Set the quail aside.

In a bowl, combine the White Sage Bread crumbs, corn, walnuts, herbs, salt, and pepper. Stir in the stock and butter.

Generously stuff each quail body and place in a glass baking dish along with the leg pieces. Set aside.

To make the sauce, put the water and squawberries in a blender and process 3 minutes. Strain the liquid through a fine sieve or cheesecloth into a saucepan; squeeze out as much liquid as possible and discard the solids.

Bring the liquid to a boil, then reduce the heat and simmer 10 minutes. Add the stock and butter and continue simmering until the sauce has reduced by about a third, about 7 minutes. Set sauce aside.

Preheat the oven to 350° F.

Spoon a generous amount of sauce over the quail to baste and place the dish in the oven. Bake 20 minutes, basting every 5 minutes.

Gently reheat the reserved sauce. Serve the quail dressed with sauce and garnished with whole sage leaves.

Serves 6

NOTE: Pink peppercorns do not taste as tart as squawberries; they have a faint taste of pepper to them. If substituting peppercorns for squawberries, add 1 teaspoon fresh lemon juice for each ¼ cup of peppercorns to keep the flavor tart.

Roast dove is a favorite game bird. It can be served with **BLACK WALNUT, WHITE SAGE, AND ADOBE BREAD STUFFING** *(left), or placed on a bed of* **SAUTÉED PURSLANE** *(above).*

Roast Dove with Black Walnut, White Sage, and Adobe Bread Stuffing

The dove is one of the few wild game birds in the Southwest seen throughout the mesas, high regions, and southern deserts. It makes a wonderful meal, especially when complemented by black walnuts, which are harvested in late summer, and white sage, which grows wild everywhere in southern Arizona and New Mexico.

BLACK WALNUT, WHITE SAGE, AND ADOBE BREAD STUFFING

½ teaspoon juniper berries (see Note 1, page 115)
1 cup water
¾ cup chopped black walnuts
2 cups Adobe Bread Crumbs (page 146)
½ cup chopped fresh chives
½ teaspoon salt
¼ teaspoon black pepper
2 tablespoons dried white sage

ROAST DOVE

6 doves or 3 Cornish game hens
2 tablespoons plus 2 teaspoons dried white sage
6 whole chives
1 tablespoon unsalted butter, melted
½ teaspoon salt
½ teaspoon white pepper

In a small saucepan, bring the juniper berries and water to a boil over high heat and cook about 5 minutes to reduce the liquid by half. Strain the liquid through a fine sieve to remove the berries.

In a bowl, combine the walnuts, bread crumbs, chives, salt, black pepper, sage, and the juniper-berry water. Stir together well with a large spoon.

Remove and discard the giblets from each bird, rinse thoroughly, and pat dry.

Preheat the oven to 450° F.

Sprinkle 1 teaspoon of the sage underneath the skins of each of the 6 birds, then fill each bird's cavity with some of the stuffing. Tuck the wings under and tie the legs together with the whole chives. Brush each bird with butter and sprinkle with the salt, white pepper, and remaining 2 teaspoons of sage.

Bake the birds in a shallow baking dish 40 minutes (for doves), or 1 hour (for game hens), until golden brown.

Serves 6

Stuffed Dove with Sautéed Purslane

Purslane, known to the Hopi as *peehala*, is a small plant with succulent, fleshy leaves that grows close to the sandy soil during the warm, moist summer months in the Southwest. Like a cactus, the leaves of purslane retain water and become juicier the more it rains. Although the entire plant may be eaten, the smaller branches and

younger leaves have a sweeter, more delicate taste than the larger stems.

In New Mexico, due to the Spanish influence, purslane is also called *verdolagas* and is widely used by many Natives during the growing season.

Purslane has a variety of uses and can be used much like watercress, which is a fine substitution if purslane is hard to obtain in your area.

STUFFED DOVE

6 doves or 3 Cornish game hens
5 dried red anaheim chiles, stemmed and seeded
2 cups Adobe Bread Crumbs (page 146)
2 cups (¼ pound) purslane or watercress
   cleaned, stemmed, and coarsely chopped
3 garlic cloves, finely chopped
1 teaspoon salt
½ teaspoon white pepper
1 tablespoon unsalted butter

SAUTÉED PURSLANE

2 tablespoons unsalted butter
3 garlic cloves, halved
9 cups (1 pound) purslane or watercress,
   cleaned, stemmed, and chopped
¼ teaspoon salt
¼ teaspoon white pepper

Dried red anaheim chiles, coarsely chopped, for
   garnish

Preheat the oven to 400° F.

Remove and discard the giblets from each bird, rinse thoroughly, and pat dry.

Soak the anaheim chiles in 4 cups water 5 minutes, until they are soft. Drain and dice the chiles.

In a bowl, combine the bread crumbs, chopped greens, chiles, garlic, salt, and pepper and mix together.

Fill each bird's cavity with the stuffing. Tie the legs together with a string or strand of corn husk. Rub the skins of each bird with butter.

Cook in a large roasting pan 40 minutes (for doves) or 1 hour (for game hens), until the birds are tender, juicy, and golden brown.

In a large skillet, melt the butter over medium-high heat. Add the garlic and sauté 2 minutes until lightly browned. Stir constantly to avoid burning or sticking.

Add the greens and stir so they are evenly coated with the butter. Sprinkle with salt and pepper and cook the greens about 1 to 2 minutes until they are soft but not too limp.

Arrange some of the greens on each plate and put 1 roast dove or half a game hen on top. Garnish with dried red anaheim chiles.

Serves 6

Colorfully patterned plates set off a dish of RABBIT, *prepared with blue cornmeal and wild mint (above), and black makes a striking setting for* POZOLE TERRINE *(right).*

Rabbit with Blue Cornmeal and Wild Mint Sauce

Rabbits are hunted frequently and eaten by many Native tribes throughout the Southwest. It is important to know that rabbits do carry disease, as do other types of wild game, and should only be killed and dressed by experienced hunters. In most states domestic rabbit is available through markets and breeders.

RABBIT WITH BLUE CORNMEAL

Tenderloins and legs of 3 2-pound rabbits (see page 130)
1 teaspoon salt
1 teaspoon white pepper
1 cup Blue Cornbread Crumbs (page 147)
8 tablespoons finely chopped fresh mint leaves
4 tablespoons safflower oil

3 tablespoons Dijon mustard

WILD MINT SAUCE

3 cups Rabbit Stock (page 130)
2 tablespoons unsalted butter, softened
½ cup finely chopped fresh mint leaves

Preheat the oven to 500° F.

Season the rabbit tenderloins and legs with the salt and white pepper. Mix together the bread crumbs and mint and set aside.

Pour the oil into an ovenproof sauté pan and sear the legs on each side over high heat until golden brown, about 4 minutes. Add the tenderloins and sear them on both sides until golden brown, about 1½ minutes.

Remove the rabbit from the sauté pan and drain the oil. Return the rabbit to the pan and place in the oven 10 to 15 minutes, until tenderloins and legs are firm to the touch. Puncture the flesh with a sharp knife; if juices run clear, the rabbit is fully cooked.

While the rabbit is cooking, put the stock in a saucepan and reduce it by half over moderate heat, about 15 minutes. Add the butter and mint and bring to a boil. Turn heat down and keep sauce warm until rabbit is cooked.

Remove the sauté pan from the oven and let cool a few minutes. With a basting brush, evenly brush the mustard onto the surface of the legs and tenderloins. Then lightly press a ¼-inch-thick coating of the bread crumb–mint mixture onto the legs and tenderloins.

Turn the oven to broil. Place the rabbit back in the oven until the bread crumbs start to brown and the rabbit is piping hot, about 2 minutes. Serve immediately with the Wild Mint Sauce.

Serves 6

HOW TO DRESS A RABBIT

If you buy your rabbit from a butcher, he will prepare the legs and tenderloins for you; remember to ask for the carcass, also, which can be used for stock. If you buy whole rabbits, you will have to dress them yourself.

With a sharp boning knife, cut the hind legs from the body of a whole rabbit. Place a leg flat on a cutting board and run the tip of the knife along the thigh bone, removing the bone from joint to joint. Repeat the same process with the other hind leg and set aside.

Place the carcass skin-side up and breast down. With the knife, cut along the backbone, releasing the meat from the spine of the lower shoulder to the upper rump. Run the knife along the ribs and down the side of the rabbit to release the tenderloin.

Place the tenderloin flat on the cutting surface and remove the silver skin and any excess fat.

The tenderloin and legs can be used for cooked rabbit recipes and the carcass for stock.

Rabbit Stock

2 carcasses from 2-pound rabbits, cut into thirds

1 tablespoon olive oil

3 carrots, coarsely chopped

3 celery stalks, coarsely chopped

3 small onions, quartered
2 bay leaves
1 small bunch fresh thyme
1 bunch fresh parsley
5 quarts water

Preheat the oven to 500° F. Place the carcasses in a roasting pan and bake 40 minutes, turning occasionally, until they are crisp and browned.

To a large stockpot, add the oil, carrots, celery, onions, bay leaves, thyme, and parsley, and sauté over moderate heat 3 minutes. Add the water and carcasses and bring to a boil over high heat, then reduce the heat and simmer 3 hours, until the stock is reduced by half. Skim the top occasionally to remove foam. Remove from the heat and pour through a sieve. Discard the contents of the sieve.

Set aside to cool. Refrigerate several hours, then remove excess fat from the top and discard. The stock will keep up to 5 days, covered, in the refrigerator and several months in the freezer. To freeze, pour the stock into ice cube trays, freeze, and store the cubes in plastic freezer bags. Large quantities of stock can be poured directly into freezer bags.

Makes 2½ quarts

Pozole Terrine with Crayfish Tails and *Azafrán* Sauce

This recipe creates a beautiful dish that is always appropriate to serve to guests.

POZOLE TERRINE
2½ cups cooked red hominy (page 21)
2½ cups cooked blue hominy (page 21)
2½ cups cooked white hominy (page 21)
6 eggs
1½ teaspoons salt
¾ teaspoon white pepper
4½ cups heavy cream
3 egg whites

CRAYFISH TAILS
4 cups white wine (see Note, page 115)
4 cups water
2 celery stalks, chopped
1 carrot, chopped
1 medium onion, quartered
2 bay leaves
1 teaspoon dried thyme
1 bunch fresh parsley, chopped
1 tablespoon black peppercorns
2 pounds crayfish

AZAFRÁN SAUCE
1 shallot, coarsely chopped
2 garlic cloves, finely chopped
1 tablespoon olive oil
1 cup white wine (see Note, page 115)
3 cups heavy cream
4 tablespoons *azafrán* (see Note, page 83)
½ teaspoon salt
½ teaspoon white pepper

In a food processor, blend each color of hominy separately 2 to 3 minutes, until smooth. Add 2 eggs, ½ teaspoon salt, and ¼ teaspoon pepper to each batch of hominy and process again 2 minutes. Adding small amounts at a time, slowly pulse 1½ cups cream and then 1 egg white into each batch. Take extra care to do this slowly, so as not to curdle the cream while pulsing. Press through a sieve to remove the skins and any lumps.

Preheat the oven to 350° F.

Fill a buttered, 5 x 9-inch glass loaf pan ⅓ full with one layer of corn puree. Pour a second corn puree layer (of another color) and top with the remaining color. Tap the terrine on a table top to level the puree and then cover with parchment paper.

Place the baking dish in a roasting pan, add 1 to 2 inches of water to the pan, and bake in the oven 1 hour, until firm throughout. Remove from the oven and allow it to cool and set. The terrine will keep, covered, in the refrigerator up to 5 days.

For the crayfish, bring the wine and water to a boil in a pot and add the celery, carrot, onion, bay leaves, thyme, parsley, and peppercorns.

Plunge the crayfish into the boiling liquid and cook 5 minutes, covered. Drain, discarding the liquid, vegetables, and herbs. Separate the bodies of the crayfish from the tails with your fingers; discard the bodies

or reserve for use in a fish stock.

Preheat the oven to 500° F.

Place the tails in a small baking pan with 1 tablespoon of water, cover with aluminum foil, and bake in the oven 3 minutes.

Meanwhile, to reheat the terrine, cut it into slices and place about ½ inch apart on a large cookie sheet lined with parchment paper. Place another piece of parchment paper over the top and bake in a preheated 400° F. oven 15 minutes, or until hot.

For the sauce, sauté the shallot and garlic in olive oil in a saucepan over high heat 2 minutes. Add the wine, lower the heat to medium, and reduce the mixture by half, about 5 minutes. Remove from the heat and strain, discarding the shallot and garlic.

Return the mixture to the saucepan and add the cream and *azafrán*. Continue to simmer over medium heat until the mixture has reduced by half again, about 5 minutes. Add the salt and pepper and stir well.

Spoon some of the sauce onto individual plates and serve with the terrine and crayfish.

Serves 12 as an appetizer

PAN-FRIED TROUT *is garnished with sautéed red chiles and garlic.*

Pan-Fried Trout with Blue Cornmeal, Red Chiles, and Garlic

While visiting Picuris Pueblo in northern New Mexico, I asked a Native American friend, Richard Mermejo, about the ancient fishing techniques that were used hundred of years before modern fishing equipment was invented. Instead of explaining how it was done, Richard took me to a local stream, where he slowly demonstrated how to fish the way the Native Americans always have.

First he twisted together long strands of horse hair, knotted the ends, and made a loop at one end. He attached the loop to the end of a long stick. He then explained how a fisherman will set the loop in a tide pool and wait for a trout to swim through the loop. When that golden opportunity arrives, the stick is jerked up to close the loop and catch the passing trout.

This technique requires great skill and patience, but remarkably it is still used by Native Americans today.

6 whole river trout, 10 to 12 ounces each
1 tablespoon vegetable oil
2 garlic cloves, finely chopped, plus 6 garlic cloves, halved
1 egg
¼ cup milk
½ cup blue cornmeal
1 teaspoon salt

¼ teaspoon black pepper
½ cup red chile powder
4 tablespoons (½ stick) unsalted butter
2 dried red chiles, stemmed, seeded, and cut into 2-inch strips

Wash each trout in cold water.

Mix together the oil and chopped garlic and brush onto each trout.

In a bowl beat together the egg and milk.

In a separate bowl, mix together the blue cornmeal, salt, pepper, and red chile powder. Dredge each trout first in the egg and milk mixture and then in the dry mixture so that each is thoroughly coated.

In a large skillet over moderate heat, melt the butter and add the dried red chiles and garlic halves. Sauté 1 minute and add the fish. Sauté the fish 3 minutes, flip over, and sauté another 3 minutes, until golden brown.

Serve hot on plates with the sautéed garlic and peppers.

Serves 6

Jerky

Drying meat into jerky is a process that Native Americans have used for centuries. In winter, when cold weather made hunting impossible, jerky provided nourishment for families. The traditional method of making jerky is an effective but very time-consuming process.

Annabel Eagle, an elder woman of the Southern Ute tribe in Colorado, recounted to me the traditional process of preparing the jerky. Her husband hunted the game — traditionally elk, venison, and rabbit — and Annabel's challenge was to cut the longest and thinnest strips of meat possible (because these dry more quickly and are less likely to spoil). After salting the meat generously, Annabel would put the strips on drying racks in the hot sun 3 to 4 days, taking them inside at night to keep the meat away from prowling animals.

Today, an easier technique that is much less time consuming has been adopted by the younger generations. I have used beef for this recipe rather than game meats because beef is more commonly eaten today.

> 1 pound tip roast, flank steak, or other lean cut
>   of beef, cut ¼-inch thick
> 1 teaspoon kosher salt
> 1 teaspoon chopped dried chile pequín
> 1 tablespoon olive oil

Cut the beef into strips about 2 inches wide and 8 to 10 inches long.

Mix the salt, chile pequín, and oil together and rub into both sides of the meat strips with your fingers. Let stand 3 hours to marinate.

If using an electric oven, preheat it to 200° F. If using a gas oven, the warmth of the pilot light will be sufficient to dry the jerky. Place the meat strips on a wire rack over a pan to catch the drippings and slowly cook in the oven with the door ajar for 9 hours, then turn the strips over and cook another 9 hours. The jerky should be medium-dry but not completely dehydrated.

Makes approximately 15 strips of jerky

VARIATIONS:

For flavor, different spices can be added to the jerky along with the oil, salt, and chile. Add ½ teaspoon oregano for oregano jerky; ½ teaspoon cumin for cumin jerky; or 2 finely chopped garlic cloves for garlic jerky.

WHOLESOME BAKED GRAINS

BREADS

Bread has been prepared and baked by Native Americans for hundreds of years. It is served as an accompaniment to most main courses, traditionally meats and stews, as well as soups and salads; it is eaten between meals with condiments such as chile sauces and a variety of jellies and is served with eggs or Indian porridge for breakfast. Bread is clearly a mainstay of the everyday Native American diet.

Before the introduction of wheat to Native Americans in the late 1800s, breads were made from ingredients, especially corn, that were readily available. Nuts and seeds were also used for bread meals. Piñons, acorns, black walnuts, and even the roots of cattails were gathered, dried, and ground into a meal that was used like flour. Native American women also made their own yeast by cooking potatoes, cornmeal, and sugar into a stiff dough that was fermented, dried, and formed into compressed cakes. This yeast provided enough leavening to make ground meals rise.

Many breads are still made from corn alone, including varieties of the tortilla, *Piki* Bread, and cornbread. But with the availability of wheat flour, many of the traditional recipes were adapted, and flour was used, which made the doughs more pliable and the breads softer and chewier. Today, commercial flour is readily available and regularly used, but many of the baking processes remain traditional, especially when the bread is baked or eaten as part of one of the ceremonial practices of the Native Americans throughout the regions of the Southwest.

One of the oldest and most unusual breads in the Native American diet is *Piki* Bread, a traditional bread of the Hopi people. *Piki* is still prepared in the same way it has been for generations, primarily by women, some of whom retreat for hours to the *piki* houses, special cabins made just for the purpose of preparing large quantities of the traditional crispy flatbread. A large, flat black stone slab is placed over an open cedar wood fire and heated until it is sizzling. Most often these stones are heirlooms that have been kept in the family for generations. With much expertise, the women spread the thin gruel made from ground corn over the hot slate in thin layers with their bare fingers. Taking only seconds to cook, the crisped layer is then peeled off and folded into light, flat rolls. This process is indeed an art form that takes patience and determination to learn.

Also commonly found in the Southwest are flour and corn tortillas. Many varieties can be found in markets today, but they never compare to the taste of homemade tortillas. The labor involved in making them is worth it when you taste tortillas served hot and fresh off the griddle.

Other breads are baked in an outdoor oven called an adobe oven or *horno*. It is a sun-dried brick oven that resembles a beehive built up from the ground. A fire is built underneath and allowed to burn down, ashes are brushed out, and as many loaves as will fit at one time are stuffed into the oven. These are baked and distributed among relatives and friends for special celebrations and ceremonies.

As in the other chapters of this book, there are purely traditional recipes here, along with modernized recipes using traditional techniques.

Indian Tortillas

Tortillas have been enjoyed by Native Americans for centuries. Women knead and flatten the dough, called *masa*, by hand, quickly patting it between the palms of their hands until it is very thin. The dough is then heated on a hot, dry griddle just long enough to crisp the outside and leave the inside moist and chewy.

Making tortillas is considered by some a form of art in itself. For the novice it can be time consuming and a bit difficult, but the reward of fresh tortillas makes the process worthwhile. *Masa* mixes are available commercially, which helps to make the process easier.

For a creative touch, designs can be pressed onto the just-cooked tortillas with a shucked corncob (or anything that will leave an interesting design) dipped in Red Chile Sauce (page 26) or Guajillo Chile Sauce (page 31). This will also add a spicy flavor to the tortilla.

Large quantities of tortillas will keep well in the refrigerator for approximately 5 days when covered in plastic. To reheat, simply warm on an ungreased griddle.

BLUE CORNMEAL TORTILLAS

2 cups very finely ground blue cornmeal

1 cup all-purpose flour

2 teaspoons salt

4 teaspoons baking powder

4 tablespoons lard or vegetable shortening

1 cup plus 3 tablespoons milk or water

20 fresh cilantro leaves, or other fresh herb

Mix the blue cornmeal, flour, salt, and baking powder together in a bowl. With your hands, work in the lard or shortening and 1 cup milk or water until completely mixed and pliable. Gradually mix in the remaining milk or water, 1 tablespoon at a time, to make a stiff dough that is dry enough not to stick to a wooden work surface or tortilla press. You may not need all of the remaining milk.

Knead the dough in the bowl 5 minutes. Pinch off approximately 1½ tablespoons dough, and roll it into a ball between your palms. Press into a flat circle on the work surface and place a cilantro leaf in the center. Roll the dough out thin with a rolling pin or place in a tortilla press between two sheets of wax paper and flatten to make round cakes, 7 to 8 inches in diameter and no thicker than ⅛ inch.

Heat a large cast-iron skillet or griddle over medium-high heat. Brown tortillas 1 at a time, about 3 minutes on each side. While the other tortillas are cooking, keep the finished tortillas warm between folded clean linen towels.

Makes approximately 20 tortillas

INDIAN TORTILLAS *are decorated with herb impressions and rolled cornhusk designs.*

YELLOW CORNMEAL TORTILLAS

Yellow corn tortillas are traditionally made from ground dried hominy or from a lime-treated corn mixture called *Nixtamal*. From this a *masa* is made and used for tortillas. It is a time-consuming process; for greater convenience, *masa harina*, a basic mix for making this dough, is available in most supermarkets. When using the commercial mix, follow the manufacturer's instructions for making the *masa*.

> 2 cups *masa* (recipe follows) or *masa harina*
>   (follow package directions)
> 1 teaspoon salt

Using your hands or a wooden spoon, mix together the *masa* and salt in a bowl. Mix until the dough holds its form. It should be a stiff but pliable dough, still dry enough so that it doesn't stick to a wooden work surface or tortilla press.

Knead the dough in the bowl 5 minutes. Pinch off approximately 1½ tablespoons of dough and roll it into a ball between your palms. Press into a flat circle on the work surface. (As in the Blue Cornmeal Tortilla recipe (page 141) you can add cilantro leaves at this point by pressing a leaf into the dough.)

Roll the dough out flat with a rolling pin or place in a tortilla press between 2 sheets of wax paper and flatten to make round cakes, 7 to 8 inches in diameter and approximately ⅛ inch thick.

Heat a large cast-iron skillet or griddle over medium-high heat, and brown the tortillas 1 at a time for 1 to 2 minutes on each side. While the other tortillas are cooking, keep the finished tortillas warm between folded clean linen towels.

Makes 15 to 18 tortillas

MASA

> 2 cups cold water
> 2 cups culinary ash (see Note, page 21)
>   or ¼ cup baking soda
> 2 pounds dried yellow corn

In a small glass bowl, mix together cold water and culinary ash or baking soda until dissolved.

Place the dried corn in a large enamel or other nonreactive pot (no aluminum, it oxidizes) with water to cover by 2 inches. Place the pot over low heat, add half the ash water, and stir well. With ash the skins of the corn kernels should start to turn yellow. Add the remainder of the ash water and stir again.

Bring the corn-ash mixture to a boil over high heat, then reduce the heat and gently simmer 2 to 3 hours, until you can rub the skins off the corn easily. Stir occasionally to prevent burning, and add more water to cover as necessary. Remove from the heat.

Drain the mixture (known at this stage as *nixtamal*), rinse in cold water, then drain again. With your hands, rub the corn kernels to remove the

skins completely. Now the *nixtamal* is ready to be ground into *masa*. Traditionally, *nixtamal* is ground by hand on a *matate* or, untraditionally, in a food processor. Process the *nixtamal* until completely ground. The coarser the grind, the coarser the tortilla meal will be. The resulting *masa* will last, covered, in the refrigerator approximately 7 to 10 days.

Makes 6 cups nixtamal, *or 3 cups* masa

NOTE: Prepared *masa* or *nixtamal* can be purchased at specialty stores or Latin American markets.

FLOUR TORTILLAS

2¼ cups all-purpose flour
1½ teaspoons salt
½ teaspoon baking powder
6 tablespoons lard or vegetable shortening
¾ cup hot water

In a bowl, mix together the flour, salt, and baking powder. Add the lard and thoroughly work it into the dry ingredients.

Place the flour-and-lard mixture on a flat work surface, making a depression in the middle. Pour the water into the well and mix together with your hands. Knead about 5 minutes until the dough is pliable. Put the dough in the refrigerator to rest 1 hour.

Divide the dough into 10 to 12 pieces of about 1½ tablespoons each and shape them into balls. With a rolling pin or tortilla press roll out each ball as thinly as possible into circles, 7 to 8 inches in diameter and approximately ⅛-inch thick.

Heat a large cast-iron skillet over high heat until very hot. (For the best flavor, flour tortillas are cooked quickly over high heat.) Cook each tortilla until it puffs and browns, flip it over, press down with a spatula to get rid of any air bubbles, and brown the other side as well. Wrap the cooked tortillas in a clean linen towel to keep warm, or reheat them in the traditional way, over an open flame.

Makes 10 to 12 tortillas

Indian Tacos

The Indian taco has become one of today's best-known Native American dishes. It is served at national fairs, intertribal powwows, and community events, both on the reservations and in urban areas.

Its base, unlike the more familiar Mexican-style tacos, is frybread, made from a light dough and considered to be of Navajo origin. Traditionally, it was prepared with lard, but now more and more people are using vegetable oil for frying.

The anasazi bean is a medium-size bean spotted reddish-brown and white. It was originally cultivated by the Anasazi people, the now extinct cliff dwellers of the ancient Southwest. For many years this bean was seldom used and hard to find, but it is slowly gaining popularity in the commercial market. It can be found in health food markets and can also be ordered by mail (see the Source Guide, page 153). If you wish to substitute, I suggest using pink beans.

1½ cups dried anasazi beans
6 pieces Indian Frybread (page 150), about
    6 inches in diameter
1½ cups mâche or arugula, washed and stemmed
1 large ripe red tomato, sliced
2 ripe avocados, halved and sliced
1 red onion, thinly sliced
1 bunch red radishes, sliced

24 golden yellow plum tomatoes, cut in half
6 green anaheim chiles
1 large red bell pepper or red anaheim chile

To prepare the anasazi beans, soak overnight in water to cover. The next day, drain the beans and place them in a saucepan with fresh water to cover. Bring to a boil, reduce the heat, and let the beans simmer until the skins break, about 3 hours. It may be necessary to add water as the beans cook to prevent them from burning and sticking. After the beans are cooked, remove from the heat and set aside. You should have about 3 cups cooked beans.

While the beans are cooking, roast, seed, and devein (pages 62–63) the chiles and the pepper. Leave chiles whole; slice pepper lengthwise into six strips.

To start building the tacos, place ½ cup cooked beans on each piece of frybread. Add ¼ cup greens per taco, followed by a red tomato slice. Add 4 slices avocado and 1 slice red onion separated into rings. Follow with radishes and 4 golden yellow plum tomatoes per taco, and top with 1 roasted green chile and 2 slices roasted red pepper or chile.

You can vary the toppings and the order in which the taco is built.

Serves 6

A modern version of the traditional **INDIAN TACO.**

Adobe Bread

This is an adaptation of the traditional recipe that is still being used by almost every Native American family.

- 1 package (¼ ounce) active dry yeast
- ¼ cup lukewarm water
- 1 teaspoon salt
- 3 tablespoons lard or vegetable shortening, melted
- 1 cup cold water
- 4½ cups all-purpose flour

In a large bowl, soften the yeast in the lukewarm water. Mix the salt, 2 tablespoons of the shortening, and the cold water together and add to the yeast mixture.

Sift in the flour gradually, beating well after each addition for a smooth consistency. You will probably have to knead in the final cup of flour.

Shape the dough into a ball, brush lightly with the remaining shortening, and cover with a dry cloth. Set the bowl in a warm place until doubled in bulk, about 1 hour.

Punch the dough down and, on a floured board, knead about 5 minutes. Shape into 2 round loaves on a well-greased baking sheet. Cover with a dry cloth and set to rise another 45 minutes.

Preheat the oven to 400° F. Bake the loaves on a cookie sheet 50 minutes, until they are light brown and sound hollow when tapped.

Makes 2 round loaves

ADOBE BREAD CRUMBS:

To make bread crumbs, simply rub the crust and/or inside of fresh Adobe Bread between your fingers to a fine crumb. One loaf makes 2 to 3 cups of bread crumbs.

Blue Cornbread

Blue cornbread can be served with soups or stews, for breakfast with any of the fruit sauces and jellies offered in this book, or with a meal as you would any other bread.

- 1 cup blue cornmeal
- 1 cup all-purpose flour
- 3 tablespoons sugar
- 2 teaspoons baking powder
- ½ teaspoon salt
- 5⅓ tablespoons (⅓ cup) unsalted butter, softened
- 1 egg
- 1¾ cups milk

Preheat the oven to 325° F. Grease a 9 x 13-inch baking pan or 2 cornstick pans.

In a large bowl, mix together the cornmeal, flour, sugar, baking powder, and salt.

In a separate bowl, mix together the butter, egg, and milk. Gradually stir the wet ingredients into the dry ingredients. Mix well.

Spoon the batter into the prepared pan and bake until firm, 25 to 30 minutes if using a rectangular baking pan

or 15 to 20 minutes if using cornstick pans. The bread should be golden and spring back when touched.

Makes 1 pan of cornbread or 15 cornsticks

BLUE CORNBREAD CRUMBS:

Cut the crust off the top and bottom of freshly baked blue cornbread and discard. Crumble the remaining bread into small pieces and put them into a food processor. Pulse until processed to a fine crumb. One loaf will make approximately 4 cups crumbs.

White Sage Bread

White sage, which grows in abundance throughout most regions of the Southwest, is an aromatic herb used in a variety of dishes. Ordinary fresh sage can also be used.

This bread freezes well, so I suggest making several loaves at a time.

2½ cups all-purpose flour
2 teaspoons finely chopped fresh white sage leaves
1 teaspoon salt
½ teaspoon baking soda
1 package (¼ ounce) active dry yeast
¼ cup lukewarm water
1 egg
1 cup cottage cheese
2 tablespoons unsalted butter, melted
Crushed roasted piñons (page 67) or coarse salt (optional)

In a bowl, combine the flour, sage, salt, and baking soda.

Dissolve the yeast in the lukewarm water.

In a food processor, blend the egg and cottage cheese until smooth; add 1 tablespoon of the butter and all the yeast water, mix again, and transfer to a large bowl. Gradually add the flour mixture, kneading vigorously after each addition, until a stiff dough is formed. Cover with a dry cloth and let rest in a warm place until doubled in bulk, about 1 hour.

Punch down the dough and knead it on a lightly floured surface about 4 minutes. Divide the dough in half and shape each part into a ball. Place the dough balls on a baking sheet, cover with a dry cloth, and let rise 15 minutes more.

Preheat the oven to 350° F.

Bake the bread about 40 minutes, until well risen, golden, and hollow-sounding when tapped. Brush the top with the remaining butter and sprinkle with crushed roasted piñons or coarse salt if desired.

Makes 2 round loaves

Piki Bread

Piki is a paper-thin cornbread unique to the Hopis. They make it in a variety of flavors and colors and serve it as you would any bread. It is made in large quantities — this recipe makes about 50 to 75 *piki* — and keeps well for several weeks, loosely wrapped and stored in a cool, dark, dry place.

This recipe is adapted, with permission, from *Hopi Cookery* by Juanita Tiger Kavena.

3 tablespoons culinary ash (see Note, page 21)
   or 1 tablespoon baking soda
6½ to 8½ cups cold water
6 cups finely ground blue or yellow cornmeal
8 cups boiling water
Vegetable shortening

Mix the culinary ash or baking soda with ½ cup of the cold water and set aside.

Put 4 cups of the cornmeal into a large, shallow bowl. Pour ½ the boiling water over the cornmeal and stir with a wooden spoon until well blended. Gradually add the remaining boiling water, stirring to make a heavy, stiff dough.

Slowly strain the ash water through a cheesecloth-lined sieve into the dough (or gradually pour in the baking soda water), stirring to blend.

When the dough is cool enough to handle, knead it by hand until smooth. Work in the remaining cornmeal, small amounts at a time. Set the dough aside to rest about 10 minutes.

Preheat a large cast-iron griddle.

A little at a time, gradually knead the remaining cold water into the dough, adding enough to make a smooth, thin batter no thicker than cream. (As you cook the *piki*, you may find it necessary to add more water, as the batter tends to thicken.)

Grease the griddle with vegetable shortening. (You'll have to regrease it after every 2 or 3 *piki*.)

Dip a pastry brush into the batter and, brushing back and forth, spread a thin film of the batter over the entire surface of the griddle; it will dry very quickly. Let the *piki* cook about 1 minute, until its edges lift away from the griddle; then gently lift it off with a metal spatula and transfer it to a tray.

Spread more batter on the griddle. As soon as its surface is dry, place the already-cooked *piki* on top and let it soften. Warming the paper-thin *Piki* Bread before folding it will prevent it from cracking easily. Fold 2 opposite sides of the warm *piki* a quarter of the way toward the center; then gently roll up the *piki* and move it to a tray. Lift the next *piki* from the griddle as soon as it is done.

Continue the procedure with the remaining batter.

Makes 50 to 75 piki

PICURIS INDIAN BREAD PUDDING, *here with apricot sauce, is found almost everywhere.*

Indian Frybread

This bread is served during some of the pueblo Feast Days, at family gatherings, and at other meals.

4 cups all-purpose flour
2 tablespoons baking powder
1 teaspoon salt
2 cups water
Vegetable oil for frying

Mix the flour, baking powder, and salt in a large bowl. Gradually stir in the water until the dough becomes soft and pliable without sticking to the bowl.

Knead the dough on a lightly floured surface 5 minutes, folding the outer edges of the dough in toward the center.

Return the dough to the bowl, cover with a clean towel, and let rest 30 minutes to allow the dough to rise.

Shape the dough into egg-size balls and roll out on a lightly floured board to a thickness of ½-inch (or thinner, for crispier bread). It is customary to use your hands, but a rolling pin can be used as well.

Place a piece of dough between your hands and pat it from hand to hand as you would tortilla or pizza dough, until it has stretched to 8 to 12 inches in diameter. Repeat with the rest of the dough.

With your finger, poke a small air hole in the center of each piece, to prevent bursting during frying.

Pour approximately 1½ inches of oil into a large frying pan or saucepan (the saucepan's greater depth will prevent the oil from splattering) and heat over medium heat until the oil is hot but not smoking.

Carefully place a piece of dough in the hot oil, slipping it in gently to avoid splattering. Cook until the dough turns golden brown and puffs. Turn over with two forks and cook until both sides are golden brown.

Remove and drain on paper towels until the excess oil is absorbed. Repeat this process with each piece of dough. Keep warm between two clean towels in the oven on low. Serve immediately.

Makes about 16 frybreads

Picuris Indian Bread Pudding with Apricot Sauce

Almost every pueblo I visited in New Mexico had a recipe for this traditional bread pudding, each one varying only slightly.

4 cups Adobe Bread Crumbs (page 146) or
    toasted crumbs from commercially bought
    bread
3 cups mild Cheddar cheese, grated
1 teaspoon ground nutmeg
1 teaspoon ground cinnamon
2 cups sugar
4 cups water
4 tablespoons (½ stick) unsalted butter

Apricot Sauce (recipe follows)
Fresh apricots, for garnish, if available

Grease a 5×9-inch loaf pan with butter or lard and cover the bottom with 2 cups of the bread crumbs. Spread 1½ cups of the grated cheese over the bread. Sprinkle ½ teaspoon of the nutmeg, ½ teaspoon of the cinnamon, and ¼ cup of the sugar over the cheese.

Add the remaining 2 cups bread crumbs and pat down so the layers are firm. Make a second layer, using the remaining grated cheese, nutmeg, and cinnamon, and ¼ cup of the sugar.

Heat the remaining 1½ cups sugar in a saucepan over medium heat, stirring occasionally until the sugar has melted. Add the water and let the sugar syrup dissolve. Add the butter and stir until it has melted with the water and sugar, 3 to 5 minutes. Pour over the layers and test with a spoon to make sure the sugar liquid has saturated the bottom.

Preheat the oven to 300° F. Bake the loaf 30 minutes until cheese has browned and sugar syrup is bubbling. Remove from the oven, place on a wire rack, and cool.

Cut into 1½-inch-thick slices and serve with Apricot Sauce. Use fresh apricots as a garnish if they are in season.

Serves 6 to 8

Apricot Sauce

I have tested this sauce with fresh, canned, and dried apricots and feel that fresh is the best; however, apricots are seasonal, and canned or dried will work also.

2 cups apple cider
½ cup sugar
18 fresh apricots, skinned, pitted, and quartered, or 2 16-ounce cans apricots, drained, or 1 cup dried apricots (see Note)

Bring the apple cider to a boil in a saucepan over high heat. Add the sugar and stir constantly about 1 minute until the sugar has dissolved. Add the apricots and again bring to a boil. Let boil 30 minutes, stirring occasionally, until the apricots are soft and only a small amount of liquid is left on the bottom of the pan. If the consistency is too thick, add more apple cider.

Serve hot or place in the refrigerator to chill. The sauce will keep 1 week in a covered container in the refrigerator.

Makes 3 cups

NOTE: Dried apricots must be reconstituted before cooking. Soak them overnight in a bowl with water to cover.

SOURCE GUIDE

Some of the ingredients used throughout this cookbook—traditional to the Southwest and seldom used outside the region—may be difficult to obtain. The following stores and produce markets are reliable sources for obtaining regional ingredients.

Bag O Beans Products Health House
2219 Oddie
Sparks, NV 89431
anasazi beans

Casados Farms
P. O. Box 852
San Juan Pueblo, NM 87566
(505) 852-2433
hominy, other corn products

Los Chileros
P. O. Box 6215
Santa Fe, NM 87501
(505) 471-6967
blue corn products, fresh chiles and dried chiles, piñons, herbs, spices, hominy.

Cookworks Inc.
316 Guadalupe Street
Santa Fe, NM 87501
(505) 988-7676
yellow and blue cornmeal, anasazi beans, chile powders, spices

El Encanto Inc.
1224 Airway SW
Albuquerque, NM 87105
(505) 822-9837
dried chiles, cornmeal products, goat cheese, chile jellies, chile powders, and ristras

Maria and Juanita Garcia's Tumbleweeds
P. O. Box 425
Keans Canyon, AZ 86034
tumleweed, culinary ash, hohoise *(Indian tea)*

The Great Southwest Cuisine Catalog Direct Marketing de Santa Fe
Joseph Montoya Federal Building
Department 2514

Santa Fe, NM 87504
(505) 323-1776
dried chiles, blue corn and other corn products, southwestern earthenware, hominy

Horticultural Enterprises
P. O. Box 810082
Dallas, TX 75381-0082
all varieties of chile seeds

Josie's Best New Mexican Foods
1130 Agua Fria Street
P. O. Box 5525
Santa Fe, NM 87501
(505) 983-6520
blue corn and other corn products, chiles (frozen, powdered, whole, and dried), hominy, tortillas, Indian frybread mix, corn husks, spices

Genevieve Kaursgowva
P. O. Box 772
Hotevilla, AZ 86030
piki *bread, culinary ash*

Lujan's Place
218 Galisteo
Santa Fe, NM 87501
azafrán, hohoise (Indian tea), herbs, spices

Monterrey Food Products
Pete Galindo
3939 Brooklyn Avenue
Los Angeles, CA 90063-1899
(213) 263-2143
salsa, chiles, cooking equipment, imports from Mexico, dried and ground chiles, spices, herbs, beans, hominy

The Old Santa Fe Chile Co.
218 Old Santa Fe Trail
Santa Fe, NM 87501
(505) 988-1289

blue corn, large variety of chiles, spices, jams and jellies

La Preferida
3400 West 35th Street
Chicago, IL 60632
(312) 254-7200
canned products including beans, hominy, salsas, and chiles; also cactus pads, corn flours, chiles (powdered and dried), spices, herbs

Seeds West Garden Seeds
Santa Fe Kitchen Garden Collection
Box 2817
Taos, NM 87571
anasazi beans, cilantro, tomatillos, anaheim chiles, jalapeño peppers, and other chiles

Southwest Herbs and Spice Co.
P. O. Box 9
Arrey, NM 87930
(505) 267-9368
azafrán, herbs, spices

Texas Wild Game Cooperative
Broken Arrow Ranch
P. O. Box 530
Ingram, TX 78025
(800) 962-GAME
free-range venison

West Central Produce
2045 Violet Street
Los Angeles, CA 90021
(213) 485-1633
cuitlacoche, squash blossoms (seasonal), all varieties of chiles

Winter Sun Trading Co.
18 East Santa Fe Avenue
Flagstaff, AZ 86001
(602) 774-2884
tuitsma, azafrán, herbs, spices, culinary ash

CREDITS

Southwestern Native American Artifacts

A special thanks to Philip Garaway of the Native American Art Gallery in Venice, California, for supplying the artifacts that appear in the following photographs:

page 32 — Salado stone matate and grinding stone, central Arizona, circa 1300; Hopi buffalo dance wand, Hopi Pueblo, northeastern Arizona, circa 1960s.

page 33 — Salado stone matate and grinding stone, central Arizona, circa 1300; Roosevelt black-on-white pottery olla, Mogollon Culture, central Arizona, circa 1250–1300.

page 37 — Hopi corn rugan kachina doll, Hopi Pueblo, northeastern Arizona, circa 1910–1920s.

page 56 — Hopi *piki* tray, circa 1970s.

page 80 — coiled Apache basket-tray, central Arizona, circa 1910–1920s.

page 92 — Hopi Ewiro kachina doll, Hopi Pueblo, northeastern Arizona, circa 1940s; San Idelfonso carved blackware pottery, northern New Mexico, circa 1950s.

page 93 — Santa Clara black plainware bowl, northern New Mexico, circa 1920s; Jeddito black-on-yellow ladles, Hopi, northeastern Arizona, circa 1325–1600.

page 105 — Coiled Apache pictorial baskets, Arizona, circa 1910–1920s.

page 116 — Tularosa plainware bowl, Mogollon Culture, north-central Arizona, circa 1100–1250.

page 121 — Navajo bow and arrow, northeastern Arizona, circa 1930–1940s.

Other Materials

I would like to express my gratitude and appreciation to the following people and businesses for allowing me to utilize their materials: original artists' work, dishware, serving platters, handmade pottery, baskets, textiles, furniture, and locations.

Bullocks, Beverly Center, Beverly Hills, California (pages 24, 49, 60, 73, and 84).

Coyote Café (Mark Miller), Santa Fe, New Mexico (page 128).

Enfield Interiors (Mona Enfield), Santa Fe, New Mexico (page 128).

Freehand Gallery (Carol Sauvion), Los Angeles, California (pages 29, 56, 57, 76, 80, 93, 105, 120, and 129).

Elaine Horowitch Galleries (Elaine Horowitch), Palm Springs, California (pages 28 and 133).

Kavena Pottery (Juanita and Tracy Kavena), Hopi Reservation, Polacca, Arizona (pages 73, 93, and 112).

New Stone Age, Los Angeles, California (pages 116 and 124).

Saint Estèphe Restaurant (Steve Garcia and John Sedlar), Manhattan Beach, California (pages 33, 40, and 149).

Umbrello Gallery (Dewayne Wout, owner, and Janell Pravak), Los Angeles, California (pages 40, 41, 48, 49, 53, 81, 85, 92, 96, 97, 120, 125, 129, 140, 144, and 149).

Umbrello Gallery (Dewayne Wout, owner, and Louise Glover), Santa Fe, New Mexico (pages 64, 101, and 117).

INDEX

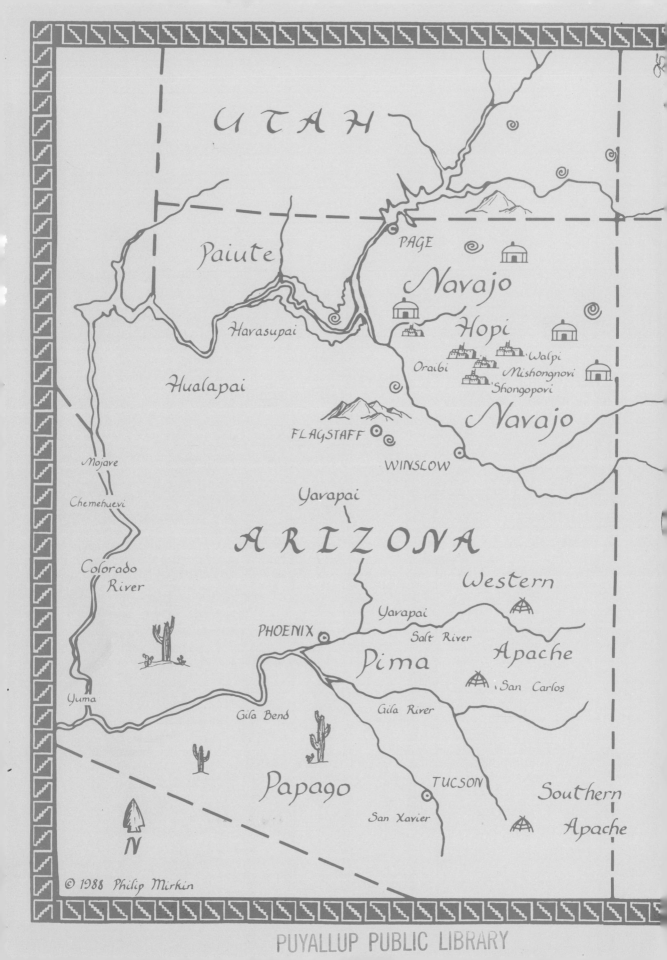